A Mystical Life

By

Peter Wright

Copyright © 2021 Peter Wright

ISBN: 9798719262581

All rights reserved, including the right to reproduce this book, or portions thereof in any form. No part of this text may be reproduced, transmitted, downloaded, decompiled, reverse engineered, or stored, in any form or introduced into any information storage and retrieval system, in any form or by any means, whether electronic or mechanical without the express written permission of the author.

Introduction

It's so strange to me that most folk rely entirely on just their five natural senses in their everyday life. These include sight, smell, hearing, touch and taste. Spiritualist mediums however believe in the extra mirrored senses (ESP - Extra Sensory Perception) which are on a psychic level. This type of sense could be utilised to enhance one's daily life in a spiritual context.

The benefits are enormous. They could bring out the real spiritual person within which leads to a better understanding of life, not only of this world but perhaps the next one too. The fact is that there is far more to us mere humans than many of us could possibly imagine.

I have always been curious about religion and the god who is, according to the popular widespread conception, the creator of the whole universe including all life. To my surprise however, I soon discovered that through my study of religions around the world that they all believe in a spirit. Yet many previous cultures had more than one god. The Roman Empire was mainly a polytheistic civilisation where many gods existed even though Judaism and early Christianity made their own paths in the first century when Jesus Christ was born.

In pagan mythology it was noted that just about anything could be seen as some type of deity (god, goddess or idol). How confusing that would be nowadays. Perhaps this is what religion or spirituality is all about, every person's right to decide who or what forms the basis for any personal beliefs or civilised structure. I personally believe that God is the universal force which includes all life forms and the wider attributes of nature.

He is omniscient (all knowing) and omnipotent, i.e. has unlimited power.

People like myself tend to look deeper into the unknown and therefore a quest for knowledge soon beckons. We tend to have many questions that we have to resolve through scientific means if possible, but in a manner that is conclusive of the truth.

Like many privileged people I had, at the age of four, an experience of 'spirit' that would eventually lead me to a discovery of immense knowledge and wisdom concerning the existence of the 'spirit world'.

I couldn't possibly envisage the potential spiritual growth of this phenomena within my life, but slowly and surely it would exact its cause to reveal a level of high spirituality within me.

As my physical eyesight eventually extinguished itself my enlightenment increased to such a level that I found myself exploring deeper and deeper into this paradoxical world of spirits. In a strange yet positive way I couldn't but help think that spirits were actually giving me a nudge or two in order to spur me on.

I believe that maybe the whole scenario came into being because of the loss of my eyesight, but whatever the reason I can now see more clearly than I have ever done before.

I feel quite comforted by the fact that I have the ability of seeing and sensing spirits. The spirit world is far closer than we could possibly comprehend.

My fulfilment came when I eventually joined a local spiritualist church where I would finally start my journey of self-development. In 2008 I began a 'healing course' and qualified two years later as an approved 'healing medium'. Yet even that wasn't enough for me because I needed scientific evidence which could be repeated time and again which verified the facts. I therefore studied the science behind spirit involvement.

The philosophy of spiritualism explains the principles of beliefs of which seven exist. They are: 1. The fatherhood of God; 2. The brotherhood of man; 3. The communion of spirits and the ministry of angels; 4. The continuous existence of the human soul; 5. Personal responsibility; 6. Compensation and retribution hereafter for all the good and evil deeds done on Earth; 7. Eternal progress open to every human soul.

These principles are a way of life, involve the science and philosophy and can be translated by all.

This book draws on my personal experiences of a spiritual nature. Some are extraordinary paranormal events and have occurred within my own house, the church that I attend, my working days or other places that I have visited.

From what I have discovered it seems that a great number of what I term natural mediums seemed to have had their first encounter with spirits at about the age of five years old.

Personally, I was only four years old and had no clue in the understanding of life at that age. Who would? Hence, my encounter was simply put aside as a memory, as a natural consequence of my life, but never forgotten.

Apparitions such as ghosts and spirits do tend to frighten most folk even if they deny it, but if we are of a good nature then we have nothing to fear.

There is a real difference between a ghost and a spirit. I shall explain this in more detail as this book progresses.

Chapter 1

My First Encounter

1958. I felt rather unsettled on this particular night. I am not sure why but maybe it was just the darkness with its eerie coldness that seemed to waft around the room. Those old terraced back houses were run down and damp which only added to the rather creepy atmosphere that I felt on that particular night. I expect that many youngsters of my age could relate to those sorts of conditions and even have had similar experiences to tell of in those bygone days.

My bed, an old iron bedstead, covered with blankets that were topped off with old large ex-army overcoats, was very warm but we had to share our bed space with our siblings because we were in the attic which wasn't very big at all. My eldest brother John seemed quite content lying in his single bed with his continuous snoring rumbling throughout our old house. My second eldest brother, Edwin, lay next to me facing the outside of the bed seemingly asleep since he appeared to be very quiet. My sisters Marie and Una occupied the last remaining space within a small alcove but seemed content snuggled up in their bed.

Suddenly my eyes became affixed to the bedroom doorway since I could clearly hear the strange creaking sound of footsteps moving up the stairs. This in itself didn't bother me as I immediately thought that it was my mum coming to check that we were all fast asleep. I had some slight concerns though when noticing how those strange dark, dancing shadows crept eerily around the walls of the spiralling staircase.

I must admit I was dumbstruck to witness a black clothed figure of a woman that I didn't recognise enter the room. Instinctively I knew that it wasn't my mom! My mom certainly did not walk with a crouched back and she certainly did not wear old-fashioned black clothing. As I watched this woman she appeared to be moving in a strange silent way, almost gliding across the floor which at the time I found difficult to understand because I knew that those old floorboards would have creaked quite loudly.

At this point I slid slowly down underneath the bed sheets, just my face and hands peeping out from underneath my safe haven that I had known since birth. As this woman came right up to the side of my bed staring down at my brother and myself, I could easily have reached out my hand and touched her face, which believe me made me cringe with gritted teeth. Yet strangely I was sure that I knew this lady from somewhere. She wore a long black gown that almost touched the floor, along with a hood that covered most of her head. Grey ruffled hair surrounded her weathered face while her skin appeared very wrinkled and dirty.

Horrifically, it suggested to me that this creature must be a thousand years old, so maybe she's some sort of witch.

Her wrinkled bony hands were clasped in front of her body which is when I saw her long, dirty yet slightly twisted fingernails. She didn't appear to have any sign of teeth in her mouth judging by the sour expression on her face.

I am sure you will understand me being a little nervous at this point, but I kept my eyes riveted on her. I'm positive though that she felt concerned or upset over something. I just unexplainably 'felt it'. Words seemed to come into my mind, words that I couldn't understand and didn't want to either. I could never forget those dark inset eyes that eerily pierced my own. It made me shiver as she stared at me for some considerable time, or at least that's how it seemed to me.

As my mind raced trying to understand who or what this woman wanted, my own eyes staring continually back at her from underneath the solace of my sheets and blankets, I came to the conclusion that she must be the witch that I had previously thought she was. I felt utterly convinced without any doubt at all. I wouldn't let her stare me out though, because for some strange reason she fascinated me. It seemed as if she was somehow attempting to communicate with me but her mouth was not moving, and I wasn't taking any chances as I thought as a child and was extremely worried that she might put a spell on me!
   She finally turned towards the window, peering downwards to the pavement, listening and observing. She suddenly turned towards my sisters' bed where I imagined that she was going to gaze down at them as well, but she seemed uninterested and returned to my bed. She seemed only to have any interest in me and my brother Edwin. Casually she turned her head very slightly back towards me as if to say goodbye, then she promptly walked through the bed as if it wasn't there, finally disappearing through the wall. One fact is for sure, you've never seen anybody move under a blanket as quickly as I did after she vanished.
   The next morning I didn't say anything about what I saw and put it out of my mind.

The Evidence

Some forty years later it was revealed that my brother Edwin had been having constant nightmares due to an incident that occurred at a young age while living at our old house in Sheep Street, Gosta Green. He told of the night when we were sharing the same bed. A horrible 'witch-like' ghost had come into our room.

I told him to stop at that point so that I could finish off the story. He sat aghast as I revealed the same ghostly nightmare in every detail, but I told him that this was no nightmare, it actually happened.

'My God,' he said, 'I thought you were fast asleep!'

'Yes, I thought the same about you!' I replied.

Well, if I ever needed proof of what occurred on that night my brother Edwin gave it to me. Little did he realise that was just the start of my visiting spirits, and to this day they still visit me in many different ways or forms.

You'll have noticed how I have referred to the lady in black robes as 'The Witch', but this has even more significance to a lady that used to come out of her house and shout at us kids to stop climbing onto the old bomb shelter.

My own mother commented that she always dressed in black Victorian style clothing of the type mentioned in my experience. Even my mom used to call her The Witch because of her continuous moaning and groaning at just about everybody and everything.

I can only assume that this was the same lady who must have passed over that evening or had already done so but came back for a visit. Perhaps she really did have some concern with us kids in her own way, but there again maybe she could just have been that same old moaning, groaning, nosey parker she really portrayed.

Chapter 2

The Differences Between a Ghost and a Spirit

The term 'ghost' seems to originate from the very ancient times of cave dwelling man. These Neolithic people even drew pictures on the walls of these caves, possibly as a means of communication or even as a religious or spiritual concept.

In our definitions we are only concerned with the paranormal influence that has always been around and has the tendency of frightening people unexpectedly.

It is important to separate and distinguish the difference between the term 'ghost' and 'spirit' since these are two very different phenomena. A ghost is what we call 'residual energy'. Residual energy is energy that is left over from the past in buildings, the atmosphere or within the earth deposits. It could be said that it is a recording or imprint of time.

These events can be very distressing particularly to nervous folk, but they cannot physically harm people although it could cause psychological problems in some cases. A ghost cannot communicate and they have no intelligence, therefore they cannot interact with anybody. They are also usually translucent in design with little or no background media portrayed. Some people such as mediums who see ghosts may have the ability of psychometry. This type of person possesses the ability of sensing the past or present through the energies of objects. This extra sensory perception is far more common than most folk realise. Residual energy may come in many forms but the most common are human, animal, or sounds. The effects of battles or sudden accidents are indications of that past life.

The fact remains that ghosts do exist and many people have seen or felt them through their own psychic senses.

Spirit.
A dictionary definition for 'soul' or 'spirit' is:
'The immaterial part of a person, the actuating cause of an individual life'.

We can say then that spirits are always with us as they are part and parcel of our existence. The 'etheric body' relates to the individual human soul or spirit that we all possess and is a duplicate copy of our physical body, yet substantially better in many ways. From birth our soul or spirit is said by many to reside within the base of our spine or base chakra until it is activated. This higher influence can then rise up and influence the very thoughts of our subconscious mind. It can interact with our conscious mind in many ways but is the intuitive function to which we all have.

Spirits, unlike ghosts, possess a higher intelligence than what we have and are able to communicate with us on a higher vibration which is attained through attunement. It is those spiritual mediums who communicate with spirits in the spirit world which proves life after our earthly death.

Have you ever felt a cobweb effect on your face? Or maybe a tingling sensation on the top of your head or face? Have you ever felt that somebody or something is watching you or even standing behind you but when you look there is nothing there? These are typical examples of an intuitive response to a spirit interacting with you or is just present at that particular time.

As I am writing this script I can hear the heavy rain outside. An intuitive thought came to me that prompted me to check the back door in the conservatory was closed.

Without hesitation I went to check this door and found that it had somehow come open, allowing rain to pour in. I firmly believe that this intuitive thought was the work of a spirit prompting me into action.

Spirits can manifest if conditions are right and the need is beneficial to us. They can interact within our dreams or through meditation, but one of the most amazing feats is that of physical or trans-mediumship where spirits can talk directly through a medium's vocal cords. This sort of mediumship is a very special link between the medium and the spirit who form a close bond of trust, discipline and confidence. It can take many years to develop and build up this bond but the forthcoming passage of knowledge that transcends is very significant to all those reading this book.

Materialisation of a spirit is often sought through the circle of physical mediumship and is most interesting on how it works. The medium will go into a trance state and as they do ectoplasm, which is an almost invisible substance, oozes from a medium's body orifices. The cheesy-type substance is gathered by the spirit and used by the alchemist to make either a full body apparition or part of the human body. This is called transfiguration. Ectoplasm can be manipulated to make a mask over a human face which signifies another resemblance of a spirit. Apart from a small red light the physical circle is practised within a darkened room, otherwise any light would destroy the ectoplasm. It begins to form around any orifice on the human body. This is then collected up by the spirit who is generally the alchemist. If there is not enough ectoplasm from the medium the spirit will look to others who are producing this phenomenon. The alchemist spirit then mixes in other compounds and uses the combined mixture for the physical transfiguration of the spirit. These could be in various forms such as a mask, part or full body, and may include rods which are used a lot in the levitation of objects such as a table. (Rods are very special within a physical circle. They are so called because they are made from an ectoplasmic substance and used to move an object as in levitation. Usually, they are seen by the medium as protruding from either the stomach or leg area of the medium and other members of the circle.)

Very often other spirits are able to use this compound in the same way, therefore increasing any knowledge or messages to the group.

Some amazing events of a spirit speaking through instruments or vessels have been heard or recorded by many mediums including myself whilst sitting within a group of like-minded people.

On one such circle meeting I had earlier heard the whispering voices of spirits in the background. Apart from one other person the rest of the group could not hear this phenomenon. It was not until some ten minutes later that a qualified medium including myself and one other member of the group distinctly heard the voices spirits coming through a digitalised table thermometer situated close to us. We were even acknowledged by these spirits when we asked if they were near us. They replied with a single rap on the end of the table, much to our delight. This particular scientific circle was aimed at a low form of physical mediumship which we conducted as an experiment.

Since spirits are of pure energy in the atomic sense, then it is easy for them to interact with anything or anybody while having the ability to come and go seemingly at will.

In the case of spirit hauntings we have to decide firstly whether the haunting is via a residual energy or spirit. If it is found to be residual energy then within time this apparition will eventually dissipate. If it is a spirit then it will depend on the occupants of the house or building as to what is to be done.

Many spirits will visit those places that hold some interest or happy event to them, yet they return to the spirit world without too much fuss. It gets a little harder though if one has to deal with a mischievous spirit.

Since there have been many recorded events of mischievous or malevolent spirits acting in ways as to cause psychological distress to some folk, then it is important that we fully understand why they do this type of thing.

Consider sudden death caused by many varying situations such as heart attack, vehicle accidents, murder or war. The person involved suddenly finds himself in a strange place where it is somewhat a shock to his mind of thought, while the majority accept that they have passed over to a different life where they accept the consequences of their own life on Earth and continue their existence with the loving spirit guiding them. It is quite reasonable to presume that a minority of these souls reject that they have passed over, while refusing to accept the consequences of the deeds of good and evil that are shown before them while they lived on Earth. The spirit helpers cannot always convince these poor souls that they are passed over, consequently they stay close to the Earth's plain. Even on a lower plain that help of progression is readily available.

We have to realise that the plains of the spirit world are

very close to that of Earth, and hence through the manipulation of the frequency allows the spirit to return back to the Earth's lower vibration for short periods of time.

When considering all of this we realise that the personality of these spirits is still the same as they had on Earth, and it is because of this fact that some spirits are mischievous in nature. These souls tend to return to a particular place of interest, for example a house and can actively make a nuisance of themselves with some effort of further manipulation of the energies available.

They could, if it becomes known to them, use psychic force to move objects, slam doors and make sounds that could disturb the occupiers of the building. Some though will do this just to get our attention because they are seeking help to free themselves from their own torment. This can be secured by means of a simple prayer towards the spirit world.

However, it does appear that hauntings dissipate over time into oblivion. Our timescales are much slower than that of the spirit world due to its frequency which is why we often think that these hauntings go on forever. This is the nature of spirits, and although only briefly written divides the terms of 'ghost' and 'spirit' in a way that is easy to understand. The light of the spirit world awaits us all and that is certain, but the pure love, knowledge and beauty of this continuous life will shine on us all, so fear not the physical death.

Chapter 3

Ghosts in the Park

As my life continued and I had experienced some strange types of psychic phenomena my working life began in earnest. Whilst at Highbury Park working as an apprentice for Birmingham Parks Department, I had one or two experiences which are featured below.

Highbury Park, Moseley, Birmingham, 1970.

I worked in a beautiful Victorian park which covered an area of about ninety acres. We had a workforce of thirteen and we all got on very well. I had been working there for a year now, relishing the outdoor life. One particular sunny spring day I was told to take the 'Atco' mower and go to the bottom rose garden. This rose garden is situated at the other end of the park close to an old rockery garden. I used a three-wheeled truck called a 'Ridley' to transport the mower and also to put the grass cuttings in. I was the only person working in that area so it was very quiet. I had turned the engine off and unloaded my mower, leaving the truck in gear with the handbrake on. To stop the engine I simply had to pull off the spark plug lead.

As I went about my work I turned round to empty the grass box and I got quite a shock. The truck had disappeared! I immediately suspected that one of the lads was playing a joke on me so I began looking for my truck. The only disconcerting thought I had was that I knew exactly where the lads were all working and that no one else had been assigned to my area.

At this point I should tell you that the truck is extremely noisy, even more so than my mower, so it would have been impossible for anyone to have started it up without me hearing it.

I eventually found the truck nearly one hundred and fifty yards away, parked on a steep hill by the rockery. I quickly ran around the area still thinking that someone was involved in putting it there. I met the old gardener who worked from his hut at the top end of the herbaceous border who told me that he was the only one working this part of the park. Going back to the truck feeling puzzled I checked it over. To my surprise I found that the handbrake was still on, the gear stick still in the same position, and the spark plug lead still pulled off. In fact, just the way that I had left it.

To make things worse Harold the foreman appeared after feeding the ducks on the pond. I related to him what had happened and asked him if there were any of the men working around here, but he categorically assured me that all the other men were working at the other end of the park. He didn't seem at all surprised at what I had told him as he told me that he had heard of similar occurrences happening before.

Broom Wizardry

One of the main jobs on a Friday was sweeping the paths throughout the park. One particular Friday I was told to sweep around the duck pond and meet up with the other men by the rockery. There were plenty of leaves lying around so I selected a good 'besom', which is a broom that is made of hazel twigs bound to a wooden stave and went about my work.

I had been sweeping for about half an hour and decided to stop for a cigarette. I held the broom in one hand as I stood watching the ducks, when to my surprise the broom flew out of my hand and hovered in mid-air about six feet in front of me. It was as if someone had taken it from me, someone who was standing in front of me, but there was no one there. The next thing I knew the broom flew through the air and landed in the pond!

Well, to be honest I didn't know what to do, think or say. The broom was out of reach, lying towards the centre of the pond. I went back to the mess room and informed the park supervisor, Ted James. He just chuckled and said, 'Don't worry, lad, that sort of thing happens all the time. It's just one the old workers from Chamberlains Estate that's doing it. It's a ghost, lad, a ghost, happens regular, quite regular.'

Terror in the Park

One day at the age of seventeen I found myself sitting in the park shelter after an argument with my father. It was a chilly night, quiet with no one around. As I contemplated my position I noticed a man walking his dog down the main driveway. Nothing unusual in that whatsoever, until he came closer to the shelter where I was sitting. For some reason I felt very nervous. Something was not quite right. It was his walking that intrigued me, he seemed to be walking on air. I watched more closely and noticed that his dog also seemed to be walking on air. He had by now got to the car park about thirty yards away from me. This car park was covered in gravel, so when you walked on it the gravel made a crunching sound. The man floated across the gravel with his dog not making a single sound.

I was standing up by now as I was feeling rather agitated. He was heading straight for me but I could clearly see that he and his dog were about a foot off the ground. I needed no second thoughts as I ran from that place, not looking back, until I was well clear of the park. This was probably the most frightening experience in Highbury Park that I had witnessed. Good job I could run!

Chapter 4

Dreams

Dreaming is a natural part of our everyday lives. The brain is an extraordinary piece of work as it deals with masses of incoming information. This information has to be stored within one's memory or immediately acted upon, much like how a computer works. At night time when our bodies are resting, our brain gets busy unravelling and storing the information that has been collected during the day. It is believed that this activity can get very chaotic as some pieces of information don't seem to be easily storable or have any particular purpose at all. To understand this just imagine performing a clean-up of your computer. It fragments bits of information and stores them in spaces that are unused. This serves to optimise the computer's memory by freeing up more space. With that in mind it is easy to see how the brain differs from the computer, so let's not compare the two together.

The trouble is with so much chaos going on with storing information we could easily have dreams that don't make much sense to us at all. A lot of our dreams seem to be confusing or even very weird in their portrayal. Images of sexuality, horror and aggression are typical types of dreams that we can all probably relate to within our lifetime, but on the other hand there are more subtle ones concerning love, peace and spirituality.
There are so many variations, yet to understand it further we should note that all of our dreams are personalised according to our lifestyle, spirituality, environment, sight, speech and emotions.

Many people around the world believe that spiritual dreams are very special since they are from a source that in itself is purely divine. I can relate to this very easily by reminding you that we all consist of a spirit via our inner body. However, not all dreams are spiritual due to the nature of how our individual brains work. Some will say that all of their dreams are defined as readable messages that are easily interpreted through a book on the subject or that it is a message from a spirit. Some religious folk even think that it is the devil working through them. Well, I suppose that's their personal choice.

In my opinion the majority of dreams are purely made up from how our conscious brain interprets our environmental situations which are through sight, sound, emotions, health and how we deal with the situation at the time. Dream analysts might give a much better description of dreams so I'll leave that up to their analytical minds.

This doesn't mean that all dreams are of the physical world because as individuals we may be on the trail of some spiritual belief. I am a spiritualist for example, but do not take away any other religious beliefs from anybody. We generally view life differently. Many though are able to interpret certain messages that come from a higher source of spirituality or vibration.

Consider the fact that when we cross over to the spirit world, otherwise known as Heaven, Paradise, Nirvana etc, we take with us our personal memories, personality and characteristics of what we were on Earth. Since we know that our inner mind interacts with our physical brain, we can easily assume that our intuitive mind is interactable with the higher vibration of the spirit world, therefore messages can be contained within our dream mechanism.

The following extracts of my diary show how we can influence our inner mind to bring forth sight, whether it be the past, present or future.

In the 1970s I clearly saw an accident waiting to happen. It must have been two weeks later when this 'dreamlike' premonition actually occurred. The scene is set in Kings Norton, Birmingham, where I saw my best friend Trevor on his motorbike coming down the road where a girls' school lay. As he drove towards the school he suddenly swerved to the right hitting the school railings awkwardly, then into a brick wall next to the entrance gates. He lay motionless after receiving what must have been a severe blow to the head and body. Fortunately, he wore his crash helmet which may have prevented him having further serious head injuries.

Shortly afterwards the school bell rang for all of the pupils to start coming out to signal the end of the school day. Adults who were waiting to take their younger children back home saw the accident happen, whereupon one of them had immediately called for an ambulance.

When the ambulance arrived and the paramedics examined Trevor, the injuries appeared serious as they did a lot of work on him before putting him onto a stretcher and lifting him into the waiting ambulance. The ambulance quickly sped off with lights flashing and sirens ringing. I learnt a few months later that Trevor spent several weeks in hospital, but eventually his life was restored once more.

The Veil 1989

Sometime before my father passed to the spirit world I had a dream which portrayed my father and myself, looking at what I thought was a great big curtain. We were at its centre where it could be parted. The next moment he had walked in so naturally I did the same. A few seconds later although was halted by somebody who held a large, open book. My father had disappeared by this time as the gentleman said, 'It's not your time yet, go back!' I did not disobey and turned around and went back.

At this time I woke up from this dream and thought, 'I'm glad it was just a dream!'

On 8th August 1989 my father had a heart attack and passed away on a bus opposite Selly Oak Hospital while out with my mom and sister Penny. I had the dream sometime before he died, but my memory concerning when I had the dream is uncertain. Yet it was before he took his transition.

I called the great curtain 'The Veil' while the said gentleman was a spirit being. This was a spiritual dream as a premonition.

Foresight 2015

Sometimes in life I wonder where and why certain things happen unexpectedly. For example, I was on a journey in a car with my friend Khalid heading to the resting tomb of Saint Abdul Wahab Siddiq in Nuneaton (UK) when he asked me if I sensed anything about the place that we were travelling to. All I knew was the fact that it was a shrine to one of the saints according to his Islamic spiritual beliefs in Sufism.

I sat there for a moment and the image of the shrine just came into my mind of which I can describe as being a building standing alone. Outside the building I also saw a star shaped pond which stood about two feet from ground level. I could also see the colour green which connected in some way to the saint entombed within the building structure. An odd moment came when I kept seeing the image of a type of headwear that is more unusual than that of a turban. All of this is quite amazing considering I have total lack of physical sight and we were still ten miles away from our destination.

Khalid seemed amazed at these revelations. As we came nearer to the shrine I could feel that we were travelling down a slight downward slope as he told me that an old car still stood in the grounds and belonged to the saint. Abdul Wahab Siddiq was well known around the Islamic territories as a diplomat who was the 'go-between' for feuding factions.

We eventually parked up in the grounds and walked to the place where the pond lay. It certainly was the most unusual pond that I have ever visited as I walked around its star shaped perimeter. We then walked up to the shrine's entrance doors and into the main seating area. Khalid described a horseshoe shaped tomb with a seat spread around its entirety. He told me that I could sit at the side where the saint's body lay in rest. Before I took up my place I was shown some oddly shaped headwear which depicted more of a coned turban.

Khalid took himself to the opposite side so that I would not be disturbed as I went into a meditational trance. It did not take long before I was seeing three spirit forms who must have stood some eight feet tall. It appeared as if the one spirit was being protected by the others. In their long gowns they appeared to be quite regal in their very colourful attire. I noticed that the one in the middle wore green as part of his clothing which helped me to understand who this spirit was. They did not stop too long, yet as I sat there in the hope that more would come to my mind little else did.

Strange but true!

20th November 2009

Before I went to sleep this night I said my usual prayer

and afterwards I asked the spirit world if I could see my father in a dream. They obviously heard my request because my dream came true. There was my dad in his younger days as a soldier kneeling on the desert floor. He was wearing his beret and uniform that was made for desert conditions. His army shorts looked a bit too big for him, but that didn't matter because just in front of him lay what looked like a straw mat strewn with papers that I believe were important documents. This didn't really surprise me too much since he was a dispatch rider for his regiment. I think that he was showing me this because it was proof of what he did in those past times, that I would realise how true this actual dream was to reality.

25th November 2009

It seems that if I ask for a particular person to come in on my dreams it usually happens. This evening I asked for my nan to come through. She was always a really lovely character who suffered silently the disease that would finally take her up to the spirit world. She was humorous, warm, very loving and often laughed heartily when I told her a joke.

The dream was quite strange though because she showed herself to be about two feet in height. I know that she was only four feet eleven but two feet? The dream based itself in the sixties when we lived in Allens Croft Road. As I came into the small grove where the house lay, there was my nan coming down the path seemingly to return to her own house in Erdington.

As she came through the gate and I was coming towards her, I suddenly sat down with my legs slightly parted on the ground. I did this as she was so tiny. I opened my arms and held them out towards her. As she came closer I picked her up and said, 'Hello, Nan,' with a big grin on my face. I then woke up and found myself smiling with delight.

Chapter 5

A Day Out

One never realises the strange events to be gained when mediumistic people such as myself go out and about. Some trips never make much of a mark on one's memory, but the following events actually took place and deserve a mention.

The Falstaff Experience 5th July 2009

I always love visiting old buildings which have charm and character. Today, along with my partner Ruth, sister Tina and my mother, we went to Stratford-upon-Avon. What a beautiful and romantic setting this idyllic small town is. Along the River Avon, opposite the wonderful theatre we stumbled upon what was an exquisite building which was known as the 'Falstaff Experience'. I had heard of this place as it has been promoted on television. Apparently, this fifteenth century building can date back as far as the ninth century and boasts some forty-two visiting or permanent ghosts.

It was impossible to resist. We had to go in and see if this really was one of the most haunted houses in Britain. On entering the solid oak beamed building with its usual white walls, I immediately picked up on a strange deathly odour. The receptionist who issued our tickets asked me if I wasn't mistaken by the building's own muskiness. I said firmly that it wasn't that sort of odour because it was separate from the usual muskiness that I have often found in old buildings. No, this was part of this building's recorded history.

We went on our way and found many small, dimly lit

rooms which had museum pieces such as a skeleton in the first room, figures of different people and objects such as writing quills, a dipping chair, kitchenware and the usual items of this building's historical interest.

The passageways were very narrow and its ceiling was quite low, but similar to other buildings of this period. I stood motionless for a great deal of the time while my group were busy studying these small rooms. I listened to what my guide (partner) had to say with interest, yet my mind seemed preoccupied with the sense that we were not alone.
Throughout our visit I picked up on three spirits in particular.
One was a young girl dressed in quite drab clothing, another was a man who seemed to have worked there, and the third a man I certainly did not like at all. This character was bad, really bad, and it took me a few minutes to get used to his presence.

Using my own mind as the telepathic link, I soon found out about the horrific facts of the murders he had committed. These had included the murder and rape of many women. I'm not sure how many but I do know that he, for some reason or other, seemed to have a hatred of females.
I took no notice of him and walked on, guided by my partner, to another part of the landing. It was to my surprise that a hand suddenly came across the side of my face and I felt as if someone had cut my throat with a knife. I turned around and nodded my head in the evil spirit's direction. Smiling at him I said,
'Is that the best you can do? You can't frighten me with your silly games so you may as well give up.' I felt he didn't like this at all and I turned from him and continued with our exploration.

A short time later he tried again. This time he attempted to stab me in the chest and bring his knife down through my stomach. I relayed this information to my party about this character and what he was trying to do. They were quite alarmed by my revelation but my sister clicked away with her digital camera to see if she could catch him on film. In fact, she clicked away every time I told her when the spirit was present.

I didn't think she would capture anything by this method but she continued anyway since in the past she has caught some orbs on film. (An orb is said to be the means of transportation which a spirit uses between two points of reference.) One should understand at this point that I felt a slight pain only for a few seconds, since it is through my psychic senses that these actions are interpreted.

I couldn't physically see this evil spirit but I could certainly pick up on his presence and his movements in those chilling corridors. We communicated through my psychic abilities called telepathy. As we progressed towards the stairs we saw an alchemist section with a mixing bowl sat on a small table in the corner of the room. Suddenly, the bowl rose up and then it came back down. My partner nervously stated, 'Did you see that? The bowl just went up into the air and came back down all by itself.' I know that my sister saw it but it was doubtful that my mother had. Once again we continued our tour and found ourselves going down a spiral wooden staircase. I was just in front of my mother, keeping an eye on her as you might say, when she seemed to lose her footing. She caught herself from falling and I gave her my hand to get her safely down the last few steps. My sister was behind my mom and clicked away with her camera for some reason. Once we were all down the steps safely Mom told us that she felt a slight pressure on her back which made her stumble. My sister certainly wasn't to blame as she was further up the staircase so we explained the incident away by saying that she had probably imagined it. Nevertheless, she insisted that she had felt a hand on her back.

We all tightened up after this incident by staying closer to one another. It was at this time that I received my third incident. I felt as if a knife had been drawn across my right ear, slicing it off completely. Once again, I felt that this spirit was very angry about something or perhaps he was just plain evil. It crossed my mind that it could have been this very spirit that attempted to push my mom down the stairs, but I kept quiet about this thought not wanting to alarm anyone.

From that point on I kept my psychic eye on this nasty spirit. We happily played some of the old-fashioned gaming machines by pulling the handles. I must admit that I did win a few old penny coins and it was a great reminder of those olden days and the atmosphere relaxed somewhat.

Finally, we finished our tour and ended up back at the reception area. I felt that since I didn't have a name for the evil spirit I would relay to the receptionist about our experience. He told us that it looked like we had encountered a certain 'John Davis' who indeed hated women and went as far as raping and murdering them in a vile manner. My group were absolutely aghast at this revelation. He also told us that many women had been affected by him as he always seemed to try and frighten them in some way. It certainly confirmed my own beliefs about that spirit and I intend to go back there at night time to find out more about the many hauntings and one John Davis in particular.

23rd August 2010

Whilst on holiday at Brean Sands, Somerset, with my mom, Tina and Ruth, we decided to go on a trip that would take us within seven miles of Minehead to visit Cleeve Abbey. It was some distance away but we enjoyed the journey nevertheless. Cleeve Abbey is a thirteenth century building known famously for the 'white monks' that inhabited the building. This magnificent abbey boasts one of the best cloisters in England. Carved angels adorn the buildings with beautiful handmade floor tiles and hand carved tiles in the dormitory which the monks had made and had kept them busy at quiet times. Restoration work was still in progress but it only appeared to be superficial work that was continuing.

I'm still amazed at how the atmosphere in each room had its differences even though the historical time period went back eight hundred years. One room in particular caught my attention rather emphatically. The room was the dormitory where the monks slept in small cubicles close to windows. As I walked through this section I became aware of much suffering, either through hunger but more so through illness.

I sat in one cubicle and through my abilities felt the terrible headache and cancerous body of one particular individual. Oh, how he suffered, yet he believed firmly the convictions of his chosen path. He later died in that same room.

Another monk had suffered from very bad arthritis and had difficulty in walking yet he did manage to, albeit slowly, even though there were no medicines to ease his pain as there are today. It came to me that this individual would use the stinging power of bees or wasps to help alleviate his pain. Many herbs were commonly used for the many ailments that these poor folk suffered.

There was another monk who had a 'club foot' which made it difficult for him to walk and work in the orchards that would have surrounded the abbey.

Yet another suffered bad back pains due to carrying sacks of flour and other heavy items. This monk would have been quite broad in
his shoulders, close to six feet tall, which would have made him quite strong in both character and build. No wonder he had a bad back because if anything needed lifting that was too heavy for most, then he would always obligingly volunteer to take the load. What a nice man he must have been.

I was glad to get out of that particular room with its dismal past, so we climbed upstairs where the atmosphere changed into one that was supremely holy yet warm and content to the individual who occupied this area. Although fairly small the room seemed to be far more comfortable, and when my sister pointed out that the occupier would have been the abbot it all made perfect sense. It appeared to me that this abbot would have lived in comparative luxury, eating and drinking good food and wine while his subordinates suffered poor health and ate meagre amounts of food. This was very common in this period of our history.

I enjoyed the afternoon immensely, this forgotten jewel of our country, especially the historical aspect of how an abbey would have gone about its daily business. I can't help think though that there is more here than meets the eye. I believe that an eleventh century building or maybe some sort of church or holy place existed in the grounds of Cleeve Abbey which has yet to be discovered.

Research at Boardesley Hall, Redditch, 4th November 2010

I went to Boardesley Hall on a cold November evening with my sister Emma and her husband Rob. There was an event laid on to support a charity called 'Chicks' who help give respite to inner city children. Two mediums looked after our group, there being around thirty spiritualist people. The evening turned out to be quite interesting as we first occupied a downstairs room which seemed to have some type of spirit activity prevalent within the atmosphere. Although members of the group seemed to sense some types of phenomena nothing concrete could be extracted. We then moved on into other rooms, but all agreed that the first room should be the room where we would hold a seance later on in the evening.

Another downstairs room was investigated as our guide wanted to see if any of the mediums could pick up anything there. I sensed the word 'guilty' but couldn't feel much more, though I did feel the pain of a gunshot in my left arm. Others within our group sensed that a ghost would occasionally show itself to which I agreed. There also seemed to be the presence of soldiers within the residual atmosphere, some may have even been wounded in battle. A group member thought that it could be something to do with the Napoleonic War, although it could not be verified. There didn't seem anything else here but our guide said he was planning to take us all outdoors later and stand opposite the window of this room.

We crept on down into the cellar where I instantly felt the presence of a female that seemed to have been kept here for some reason or other. She appeared distressed, crying as if in pain. Other members of the group seemed to think that this young lady was actually trying to study, write or was learning to read. I believe that she was being punished because I could sense a certain pain within her.

We walked further into the cellar where I recognised the presence of a young man called Joseph, Joe for short, while the presence of a female energy also made herself known to me as Mary. I had to laugh when I sensed that these two individuals were lovers who used this cellar for their illicit affair.

I could even sense a particular area of the cellar where their passion would have taken place. The female seemed to be a maid while the young man seemed to be some sort of footman but also dealt with the horses in the stable. Ralph (medium, leader of the group) also felt the name Joseph and the presence of a female spirit.

As we returned to the main house we climbed upstairs where the presence of a woman and children were noted. It appears that a certain lady is often witnessed in this area while the sounds of young children could clearly be heard playing their games. We attempted to get the children to interact with us but there was no communication forthcoming. However, I could feel one child in particular who actually touched me then vanished. She seemed to have passed through the cause of illness to which was later confirmed.

Eventually, we went outside the house to the spot opposite the window of the room we had previously visited. The whole atmosphere of this area seemed positive with death. This turned out to be rather interesting when Emma sensed a hanging from a tree that was no longer present. I personally sensed many people in this area, some running about but mostly the overwhelming power of a convicted criminal or criminals seemed prevalent. The hanging was confirmed by the guide and I congratulated Emma for picking up this information.

After a short break we returned to the first room we had visited and settled down to form a seance with myself positioned in the middle of the circle. I wasn't sure what would happen, but when the medium (Sharon) asked for any spirit presence to come forward I certainly surprised myself. It seemed as if I went into a light trance where a spirit named John came through me and started speaking.

He seemed quite amused with our antics and could not understand why we were in his house. He said that he was the master of the house and was having a drink of good brandy with the bishop of the local monastery. These two individuals seemed very close friends to me, possibly through some sort of acquisition of contraband. One of our group asked if they had smuggled any contraband to which John replied, 'Mind your own business!' At this point the two pals went quiet and backed away and said no more. My link had been broken but it was such a thrill personally to have this wonderful link of a spirit talking through me.

Other names of Harry, Mary, Elizabeth and Harold were sought by the group but little else could be extracted. It was confirmed later on that the master of the house was indeed a Sir John and many of the names mentioned also appeared in our guide's list.

The last seance came at the end of the evening with all thirty of our group taking part. Ralph and Sharon conducted this but it seemed as if the links with us were being overshadowed by the influences of past events and sadly the seance had to be abandoned. This wonderful house produced some interesting phenomena and can be accepted as being haunted by its own past. It's a pity so many of these beautiful houses are spoilt by the modern conversion of office workspace which spoils the unique atmosphere of olden days gone by. Yet to see so many friendly faces of the group which included Ralph and Sharon was simply magical.

Soul Rescue, 9th November 2010

Soul rescue is generally administered by a medium whose job it is to help alleviate the sufferings of a trapped soul.

As a spiritualist our church often has requests to help when hauntings start to materialise. Sometimes there is a need not only to understand the situation going on but the individual spirit who is actually calling out for help. Helping souls who have passed over from this Earth is very rewarding, not only to the lost soul but to the occupiers of the premises as well. While the occupiers are generally frightened by the mysterious noises and goings on within their property, the lost or trapped soul find themselves in a dismal loop of self-consciousness, possibly brought on by their own state of mind while living on this Earth. Many are in this position due to denial, sudden death or the retribution factor of their own follies or evil deeds. Others fall into combinations of the above, but materialism, poor spirituality, ignorance and a distinct lack of good knowledge may also contribute to the position that they find themselves in.

Although the spirit world will eventually help all of these sad souls, the focus must lie within them to identify and accept their misgivings for themselves.

The example shown below has the hallmarks of a spirit in denial of his own past and his present position within the spirit world. This may mean that he cannot accept the fact that he has passed over to the paradise land of the spirit world, or because he is still grounded to the physical Earth's plain due to his materialistic mannerisms. Whatever the actual reason for his present position, he would have been making life for the house owners quite disturbing. Something needed to be done for these people.

Relatives of this couple recognised the stress that the phenomena was causing them and this eventually resulted in them contacting our spiritualist church.

My colleague Chris picked up the challenge and we went along to the couple's house. When we arrived it seemed quite obvious that the lady in particular was besides herself, finding it very difficult to cope with the unnerving stress of this entity. We chatted for a while to see if there was any history on the deceased spirit that may help us in our investigation.

This resulted in them revealing that although not a lot was known about the former occupier, he did like football and lived alone with his dog, possibly having an ex-wife in the past. Apparently, he died in his bedroom but was not discovered for some time. His dog must have got quite hungry because when he was found the dog had started to eat his corpse! Alarmingly, if that wasn't enough, his body was accidently dropped down the stairs by the medics. Would this be the cause of a haunting? It certainly wouldn't have helped, but generally this would not be a good enough reason or a strong enough motive to lead to a haunting.

We felt it was important to establish whether the phenomena was just the result of residual energy or a disillusioned spirit. We soon realised that the latter seemed most prevalent in this case. Although a pattern seemed to exist, the energies of the atmosphere presented a different story.
To understand this one should conceive that residual energies are deposited by former occupiers who may have had a troublesome past. In this case it seemed correct because according to the present owners there certainly was a lot of animosity within the dwelling. Add to this the

actual presence of the spirit and we have differing vibrations present.

The couple told us that the entity would come from his bedroom, crash into what sounded like a TV, come down the stairs quite heavily and into the living room. Objects would disappear completely and then materialise in a different room or place, but in some instances some objects would not return at all. Doors would be heard slamming while a ghostly apparition could be sensed by the distressed couple. It did not seem to bother the husband, but the lady had reached the point of having to flee the home a few times in recent months.

As we chatted in the living room I could feel the pull of an energy which wanted us to go upstairs to a particular bedroom. I told them this and Chris and I went up the stairs followed by the owners.

How strong that magnetic energy felt as we climbed those stairs. When we got to the top, I knew exactly which room I wanted to go into. On entering, it felt as though I had hit a dense brick wall of a most unpleasant energy. I could clearly sense the presence of a spirit in the room and it came as no great surprise when the lady of the house refused to enter the room since she feared the obnoxious atmosphere. Chris had followed me in and he too could feel the presence.

As Chris moved about the room he pinpointed a particular area where the energy was at its greatest. I readily agreed. The amazing thing was how cold it appeared in that room considering the radiator felt very warm. The spirit stayed in the shadows as Chris and I attempted to communicate with him, but it didn't seem at all willing to communicate with either of us. However, since I am quite sensitive to those showing signs of illness, it came as no surprise to feel a sharp pain within my chest area which resembled that of a heart attack.

Our host eventually ventured into the room noticing how cold the room felt. She agreed with Chris that the area where she felt most disturbed was the same area where we felt the greatest energy.

We continued investigating the other rooms upstairs but apart from the master bedroom all seemed quite normal. The master bedroom concerned me slightly since a different kind of energy seemed to be present by a wardrobe. I kept quiet about this because I could not quite understand why this static energy prevailed an eerie presence within a singular area.

I wondered if this could be 'the doorway' which the spirit used to enter into the property. Although some paranormal researchers believe in the existence of a 'doorway' or 'portal', I'm not entirely convinced that any spirit needs such an entranceway to enter our atmosphere. It is true that a spirit would need to lower his vibration in order to interact with us in the physical world, but that does not necessarily mean that a special point within the atmosphere is required.

Revealing such thoughts while the owners of the property were present could cause them even more worry, so being considerate I kept these thoughts to myself. I rather suspect that my colleague Chris had also picked up on this energy source but decided to keep quiet for the same reason.

Returning back to the first room that we investigated we chatted about the options that would be necessary in order to evict this poor disillusioned spirit. While Chris suggested that a seance was probably our best option, I couldn't help but think that this was not necessary. However, I happily went along with this proposal.

The female owner at this time seemed a lot calmer and agreed to us performing a seance as soon as possible. Chris said that it would be best to ask his mother Pat to join us as soon as we could arrange it. She was an excellent well-known medium and one whom I held in the highest regard.

While travelling back for the return visit Pat started to perceive information pertaining to the spirit in question, describing some details of said spirit. She correctly described his characteristics along with other intriguing information. We were even more delighted when we walked into the house to be told how much calmer and peaceful the whole atmosphere of the house had become since our first visit.

The lady of the house also stated how the noises had calmed down to an acceptable level and that she no longer felt as frightened as she used to be. This was of course wonderful news, but it does show that the mere presence of spiritual people like ourselves can provide an influential calming effect within the atmosphere.

After a lovely chat with the now happier couple we decided to check out the upstairs rooms, since mischievous spirits may just be taking a break to give a false impression that they have left. I have found that this is not unusual.

However, Pat and I did not feel that the spirit had completely moved on because we could both feel his presence and energy. Furthermore, when we went into the master bedroom we could sense an unusual energy fanning out from the direction of that wardrobe. Pat remarked that this could be the area where the spirit enters into our atmosphere. That confirmed my thoughts from our first visit.

Venturing towards the wardrobe I put my hands onto one of the wooden doors only to find that it was colder than the other door. I beckoned Pat over to feel for herself and she agreed with my findings. The temperature of this door would have been about ten degrees lower than the other one.

From this point on Pat, myself and the lady owner joined hands at my request and Pat gave out a prayer towards the spirit world to intervene with helping this poor spirit back to the light. I also asked for the healing angel to help heal the spirit in question. We also suggested that the lady owner put a lighted candle close to the wardrobe which would help seal up any entrance and give a little harmony to the bedroom itself. The use of burning incense could also be deployed if the lady so wished.

We left that house feeling that we had done a good job and that the owners could be more at peace in their home than they had previously felt. If a haunting persists we generally hear about it, yet on this occasion no correspondence came forward. I am quite satisfied that the spirit in question achieved his goal and went peacefully back into the loving arms of the spirit world.

The Creaky Cauldron, Stratford-upon-Avon, 19th May 2013

I was very pleased to receive an invite to the ghost hunt at the Creaky Cauldron, which is a mid-fifteenth century Tudor manor in Stratford-upon-Avon. I had heard that it was a very active place with several hauntings going on. Once again, I had learnt about it via Jenny and her charitable work. I knew a few of the people that attended this group which always makes it a better experience.

We started the walk around with the lights on and guided by Dave, the owner of the manor, who knew of the history behind this inspiring place. He did mention that the building used to be a very large hotel that stretched the entire length of the road in the past. The place was assumed to be about four hundred and eighty years old but apparently there had been buildings on this site since around 1140.

The group, around thirty, divided into two separate groups, one going upstairs and the other (which included myself) to the first floor.

The first room we entered was quite small with benches around two walls and a single chair. This chair, we were told, was one that we shouldn't sit on as it was believed that it belonged to a strong entity that was attached to it. One of my colleagues, Mandy, sat on the chair and she immediately went into a trance in order to channel the spirit. A male came through to her and told us all to 'Get out!' No other information could be obtained from the entity.

I sat on one of the benches and soon started to feel breathless which I found to be quite amusing. Of course, I relayed this information to the group. Dave asked if I was sitting in the corner, which of course I was. Perhaps this was significant but I didn't pursue the question.

Some of the rooms had a peculiarity about them. It was as if they weren't in the correct place. I found a rather large fireplace in one room but the room itself was far too small to have a fireplace of this size. I mentioned to Dave the room should be at the front of the house facing the main street and it should be much bigger in size.

Dave confirmed that I was correct because the building itself had gone through a lot of changes which included adding rooms to the front of the house. Apparently, the main road was more like a lane in the past, therefore in modern times it became what would have been the back of the house.

As we continued the tour I couldn't help but feel that there was another secret room somewhere within this manor house. I made my feelings known to the group because I thought it felt rather sinister.

This old house made me feel confused because of its very small passageways, undulating floors and ceilings of varying heights. Indeed, this house had gone through many transformations in its lifetime.

One very small room had a manikin that stood in a corner with a treasure chest on the floor. Apparently, it is believed that this manikin had been known to move its head while the chest on the floor contained evil items of the devil within it..These are generally black magic items. A black framed mirror adorned the wall.

This room felt quite obnoxious, the sort of atmosphere that one would not be happy to be left alone in. It was very strange that in every room the atmosphere felt different and the varying temperature added speculation of an ominous presence. After our initial walk around which took about two hours, we all gathered together in the ground floor tearooms for a cup of tea and a sandwich. It was here that I noticed a spirit lady walk past me holding what looked like a wicker basket that contained fragrant herbs. The aroma of those herbs was also detected by a couple of the women who also commented on the lovely fragrance. She wore a bonnet of white cotton, a long bluish dress and a cream shawl round her shoulders. She was in her mid to late twenties and her period of dress seemed to suggest the late sixteenth or early seventeenth century.

My senses were working overtime as I sensed another time period which was a little before the spirit flower lady and was when Oliver Cromwell and his parliamentarians were engaged with the royalists. I spoke out telling our guide that many horses were once tied up outside and that 'tin heads', meaning Roundheads from Cromwell's army, must have been stationed in this building. A sense of royalty also seemed to be prevalent as a residual energy somewhere in the building.

Perhaps one of the most sordid insights that I had received was somebody being bricked up within one of the walls. Certain noises of children rang out to some of us, but I also picked up on some secret sect that used a particular room for their meetings. It felt almost religious but that could have related to just one person of this sect.

Once we had finished our break we split into two groups with one group on the second floor while our group investigated the first floor. We sat in a room that had benches around the sides and a single Harry Potter style chair which had its backrest formed almost to a point. A replica talking hat of the same theme also lay on this chair.
We tried a seance without much luck, so I asked if anybody would like to sit on the chair. They declined and asked me to sit there instead, so I readily agreed. I did not consider that this chair held any real secrets, but the room and the atmosphere certainly seemed active.
Going into a meditation I soon realised that a voice was attempting to talk through me. Mentally I allowed this to happen but kept a conscious control over the proceedings. It wasn't a surprise when the voice of an Irishman came through, telling the group to go away. Apparently (I do not remember this part), he then got abusive, especially with the ladies of our group. He swore at them telling

them that they were 'f!!king whores!'

This didn't bother the group because they were intrigued to know who he was. The Irish spirit told them that he was McGilligan. He then suddenly, or should I say **I**, lifted **my** head and stared with a frightening look directly at the first female of the group. Another female who was sitting next to the first also received the same warning glance which made them both feel uneasy.

I remember these ladies talking to me as the spirit man backed away, but I heard them respond with a simple 'yes'. It took a few moments to come back to reality, but the experience did not bother me. After the incident we chatted amongst ourselves as the other group made their way down to the room next to us.

The group decided to go upstairs and once again attempt a seance. Unfortunately, little activity could be deemed from this room so a colleague and I went back into the room with the manikin. The atmosphere was so thick that one could cut it with a knife. I felt as if some sort of black magic may have taken place here but perhaps that was because of the black mirror, the devil's chest and that overwhelming figure of a manikin. It is fairly easy to suggest that a witch might stick pins in this figure, casting spells onto some unfortunate victim. It was also stated that by looking into the black mirror one could watch your own face change into quite frightening features. This is known as scriing.

Later we went downstairs to join the group on the first floor where we were invited to join in their seance. We all stood in the centre of this room but strangely it made many of us feel almost seasick. We felt as if we were actually on board a ship that was rolling from side to side on a tempestuous sea. One can imagine the effect it had on many of us. Indeed, quite a few of the group had to sit down as they felt so ill.

We continued the seance despite these overwhelming feelings of seasickness that many of the group were feeling. As we continued some of us felt the presence of a man walking around our circle looking for a weak link in the chain where we all held hands. Eventually he did find a person he could influence, and that person stood directly to the right of me.
She felt quite sick by his oppressive presence and had to sit down. The malignant form then seemed to vanish and everything appeared to settle down and become calm once more.

Little else happened in the room and so we called it a night. After all, it was now four in the morning.
We returned to the tearoom and our guide gave us the verdict on how we all did. As far as my own instincts went I wasn't surprised by Dave when he told me that everything that I had told him was perfectly correct apart from the Irishman's name which could not be verified. The secret room did exist and children were apparently kept there in preparation for the slave market. A secret society, one of a religious order, used a room for their secret meetings. Two young children were found bricked up in one of the walls because they had died from the plague. It is told that if the owner had taken out their bodies then those collectors were instructed to lock up the premises with everybody still inside. This was to ensure that the plague would not spread.

The room where a lot of the group felt seasick was caused by the room being built with the floorboards of a ship. It is suggested that a member of the household of King Louis XVI stayed there.
One thing that had escaped my senses was that a

murder of a young child had taken place. Apparently, the poor soul had been pushed down the stairs by a lodger. The lodger not surprisingly had run away. Another man happened to come across the child's body but was mistakenly perceived that it was he who had murdered the little girl. He was tried, found guilty and sadly hanged for a crime that he had not committed. Although screams were heard by myself and other members of the group, none of us picked up on this vile murder and the injustice that ensued. I can only presume that because there was a lot of activity surrounding this building, plus the different atmospheres and temperatures, it was perhaps not surprising that we missed this important event.

All in all the Creaky Cauldron was an exciting venture and I would put this building at the top of my list of the most active places that I have ever investigated.

Chapter 6

Healing

METHODS

Contact Healing

Contact healing is the main type of spiritual healing since we have physical contact with the patient. It is on a 'high level' which is made possible by the mind and thought. It is a blending of souls.

When the healer places his/her hands upon the body of the patient the energies are transferred via the hands.

Some healers will just use their palms for this transference while others may use just the fingers or a combination of both. It doesn't really matter providing we have contact with the patient.

On a personal level and because of the fact that I am totally blind, I prefer to hold the hands of the patient because they always tell me how warm and comforting this feels. Many also tell me how they feel the energy's warmth go up their arms and into the rest of their body. I believe that this shows absolute proof that the administering spirit's healing energies are being channelled successfully. A good harmonisation with a spirit is very important.

If the patient is attending their first healing session and are nervous then the spiritualist healer will need to reassure them that all they have to do is listen to the meditative music being played. In order to aid relaxation, we should apply the sort of comfort that is conducive of inspiration and love to create a happy and relaxed atmosphere.

It is up to the healer to create this reassurance even though the patient will have already been told what to expect and how the healing works.

Distant Healing

Distant healing occurs when both patient and healer are in the same room or building but when no physical contact takes place. As in absent healing, distant healing is much the same. This means that distant healing is through prayer and thought. It is recognised that distant healing can be very effective from the healer's point of view since they don't need to move around the patient or be put off by the patient's own movements of discomfort. This link of attunement can be as powerful as other methods because there are no physical obstructions.

Absent Healing

With absent healing both patient and healer are absent from each other. The healing takes place through thought and prayer only. It could be more effective if both healer and patient were to set up a particular time for healing to take place so that both can be in a spiritual mindset. This synchronisation would increase the link between the three spirits, thus making it a stronger one. Obviously, any timescale would need to be arranged but not necessarily by the healer, since a message could be through a friend or close relative.

In a lot of spiritualist organisations there is usually a healing book available for anyone to insert the names of people who are in need of 'special thoughts'. Other ways include church meetings where the minister asks the congregation to give thoughts of healing to particular people. Positive thoughts like this works fine.

Magnetic Healing

What a beautiful way to use your psychic awareness. Most healing mediums would say that they know the particular area of imbalance before the patient has told them what is concerning them. A simple handshake by a healing medium may also indicate the problem, but it should be noted that this method is not spiritual healing. It is on an intuitive or psychic level and includes the 'aura fields' which are in themselves electromagnetic.

On the platform you may often hear a medium say that there is a lot of energy here or that the atmosphere is wonderful, but it means that the people within the congregation are giving out this powerful state of 'well-being'. Individuals are often targeted for their bountiful energies, while others may have little to give. It depends on a person's emotional, physical and spiritual state at the time.

Here is a prime example of electromagnetic phenomena:

At a closed circle that I attend we, the participating students, were told to go into meditation and make a link with a spirit in the hope of receiving a message. I always send my thoughts out to people in need of healing as I did on this occasion. There wasn't a particular link with a spirit at the time but what I noticed through my third eye astounded even my greatest expectations. I became aware of a force field above my head. Naturally, I looked up to see that just above the heads of everybody in the room this strange, wonderfully coloured sea of waves stretched across everybody that was present. I do not believe that they were aware of this fantastic phenomenon as a lot of them were still learning the basics of mediumship. In this group I appear to be the only person who had this particular psychic gift.

The whole area became a kaleidoscope of colour, gently rolling back and forth. I noticed though that a few people had distorted and dull aura fields which were emanating from their presence. From this I distinguished that these people were the ones who needed spiritual healing.

When the room returned to normal I set about sending distant healing through thought and prayers to those particular people.

It occurred to me on observation of this wonderful vision of colour that the source of all this energy actually radiated from around my own physical body and that of all others. It gave me the insight that all living things have this energy field radiating from them. It also gave the ultimate proof to me that I do indeed give out a good energy field, although I could not believe the amount of energy within it. This has been confirmed many times by many people who say what good energy they feel I give out.

The rest of the evening saw me giving messages to two people and being quite accurate with these messages. It was a great honour and certainly a wonderful privilege to have witnessed this beautiful spectacle. I have seen auras before but never on such a grand scale.

Sometimes we have to answer some incredible questions such as, how do you know when you are attuned with a spirit? My simple answer is that the energies begin to flow through my own body, then into my arms down to the palms and fingertips of my hands. It's all about reaching one's true potential.

This is by no means easy for most healers. Time, patience and experience along with a high level of dedication to the work helps tremendously. Sympathy and a listening ear help the patient's anxiety, and as experience grows a better understanding of the patient will add to the healing medium's potential. There are many obstacles in life that can keep the healer back, things such as illness or because the state of the healer's mind isn't as it should be. If however I feel ill or am not in a fit state of mind, then I would simply leave healing alone until I am able to facilitate it with body, mind and soul. I could use the term 'we're only human' but it is up to every individual spiritual healer to maximise his or her potential.

We are not invulnerable to a patient's desperate state of distress or illness, especially if their disease is one that is easily caught by others. On many accounts I have witnessed healers becoming emotionally distressed themselves and not being able to continue healing. Sometimes we have to rise above these situations and not get personally involved with every case, although most healers are very sensitive themselves which can cause difficulties. Many would say that 'this is life' and we have a deep sense of duty of dedication, sympathy, empathy, sincerity and a deep concern of others which are part and parcel of our qualities as healers.

When I have completed my initial link with the healing spirit I feel as if I am in an unknown world. It is one that is so beautiful and so tranquil that it possesses a uniquely loving feeling of calmness.

Yet to me it brings about a feeling of wantonness that is so special that sometimes I wish I could just stay there in this beautiful paradoxical world.

Healing Experiences

One never knows quite what to expect at healing services so the following examples must be seen as part of the healing medium's journey of self-development.

This section shows more examples that have occurred to me during rest periods of healing.

31st March 2009

Positive attunement is always essential but this evening I put my heart and soul into it. The energies were absolutely wonderful and extremely strong, so much in fact that my fingers were positively bouncing off my patient's hands. Once the healing session had been completed I asked the patient how she felt. She replied that it was great but noticed how my fingers were vibrating with some sort of electric charge coming out of them. I assured her that certainly the energies from spirit were very strong, but this is a normal process that happens. She wanted to know if other people felt these strange but quite lovely sensations. I told her that many patients usually feel something.

I perceive though that since there were two healers attending this lady the energies became more amplified towards her.

I always tend to sit at the front of the patient because I become more relaxed and better focused. The fact that there were two healers added a lovely conception to the art of healing.

The healing session for the evening had now finished.

I decided to stay within the confines of the 'healing room' in order to give prayers to the administering spirit. An administering spirit is a high, divine spirit and I would spend some time meditating without anybody else being present.

As I sat quietly I noticed the unmistakable squeaking sound of leather shoes that were moving around the room. These sounds didn't really surprise me too much since before the healing session had begun I had noticed that a spirit was sat at the back of the room. This is quite normal but usually I take little notice.

I started to wonder who this spirit was, therefore I asked him to come closer to me. He obliged by walking around the area where I was seated. He then moved off towards the exit door. He seemed to stand there for a while as if he wanted to know who was out there. Perhaps he had expected more healers to come in, but I knew that the healing session had finished.

Because of my blindness I always have to wait for someone to come into the healing room to guide me out. Maybe he thought that they had forgotten me, but for whatever reason it seemed quite strange. He moved away from the door as one of my colleagues came in. I took the initiative by asking her if she could see anybody else in this room. She replied that nobody had entered since the healing session had finished. I then told her what had transpired in the last few minutes. She seemed very surprised at what I told her.

When we left the healing room and entered the tearoom for a well-deserved cuppa, the healing leader came in to see how I felt things had transpired that day. I replied that I felt the healing session had gone very well but proceeded to tell her of my experience when I had been left alone in the room.

She replied very frankly, stating that she had seen the same gentleman and so had our president. She stated that he sat at the back of the room quite frequently. He had also frightened her once because she had entered into the room to turn the lights off at the end of the evening and had seen him sitting there. She had mistakenly thought that he was one of the patients.

We came to the conclusion that he must have been one of our old members who had come back to the place that he loved. He can come back any time he likes as far as I am concerned as it's nice to meet new spirits.

This was indeed a memorable day for me because it was the day I learnt that I had passed my written examination called Healing Certificate One (HC1).

12th May 2009

Henry seems to arrive here most Tuesday evenings but now he comes to me when I acknowledge his presence. He now strokes my shoulder to show that he is here even though he made me jump while I was in the middle of healing. I wasn't even thinking of him but when I received the stroking sensation I actually thought it was the signal from my colleague that healing with this patient was finished. Since I didn't hear her move towards me I carried on with the healing process.

17th May 2009

Today I felt slightly taken aback when I sat opposite a patient who I was healing. My fingertips were resting on the patient's hands but for a reason I can't explain I suddenly had a very vivid vision of pure holiness. I have to stress that my mind and thoughts were at the time in a passive state (from an active to an inactive mind). It seemed that out of nowhere stepped this older looking gentleman who had long golden hair and was dressed in white robes that stretched down to his ankles. He also carried a long wooden staff by his side. The vision then turned around so that I was looking down upon my own presence, the patient and this highly charged spiritual being.

At this time I clearly saw him laying his left hand on my shoulder, while the other hand grasped his staff that pointed in an upwards gesture.

It occurred to me that even though I was looking down on this very spiritual scene that a thread of white energy kept me positively linked to my own physical body.

I couldn't help but notice how quickly this smothering mass of white light covered not only myself but also the spiritual gentleman and the patient opposite me.

The spirit seemed to be looking upwards, holding his staff high in the air. I don't know why but I tried to do the same only to realise that I couldn't. Perhaps it was the 'power of the energy' that had me in its control as it smothered all other thoughts.

It was at the same time that this vision was occurring that I felt a flow of energy that dissipated down my arms, through my hands and into the patient's body. The whole scenario seemed to last for ages until I became conscious once again and the healing session came to its end.

I can only believe that the spirit gave me an insight into how they work with us during our spiritual healing sessions.

I have to admit though that this strange phenomenon has only happened once before while I have been conducting healing sessions. This one however has to be the one that is uniquely wondrous, so spiritual in design and was truly magnificent in nature.

I spoke nothing of this to my patient although I did ask her how she felt afterwards. She replied that she thought how warm my hands had become and how she could feel a sensuous tingling running up through her arms and even into her body. Well, that figures I thought, so I just smiled back at her. She eventually stood up and told me how good she felt and what a wonderful warm, loving and inviting place the church we were in really was.

I believe that this night's healing session was particularly absorbing for myself, but I must say that this type of vision during a healing session is very rare. Nevertheless, if the spirits want to show me something, who am I to argue?

22nd May 2009

Once again after a healing session had finished I became aware of a presence within the healing room. The footsteps confirmed who this was and I felt privileged to be close to this spirit. This time I invited him over to where I was sat. I heard his footsteps come towards me but then another one of the healers walked in to collect me. I told her what was happening so invited her to sit with me to see if we could establish communication with him.
Although we couldn't hear his footsteps, we certainly heard his movements nearing our position. Just then my colleague jumped as she felt a hand upon her head. I asked her if she sensed this spirit and she verified this. She said the name 'Steve Henry' was a possible name for this spirit but this didn't sound quite right to me.

I also picked up on the name of Henry but not a surname. I had the impression that he seemed to have an authority that was somehow connected with our organisation. We assumed that he could have been a member at our establishment, but one thing for certain was he had a great interest in our healing work.
It seemed as though he wanted to observe how we worked as healers and I think he was quite happy with what he saw. Another healer chanced to walk into the room and sadly we lost the link.

We chatted with the group of healers with one suggesting that this spirit could be Henry Needham. Apparently, his
picture used to hang on the wall in our church. It made perfect sense to me so I asked who this spirit was in real life. I felt a little surprised to learn that he was one of the founders of the spiritualist movement in our district. That just about summed it up nicely for me. The fact that he showed some form of authority seemed to fit the puzzle together. I went home feeling uplifted yet determined to find out more about this man, Henry Needham.

29th August 2009

The wonderful thing about spiritual healing is that it serves not only people but animals of all descriptions. It so happened that I bought a couple of terrapins for my partner Ruth who had always wanted terrapins, so it came as a nice surprise to walk into a pet shop and find that they were selling small yellow bellied terrapins. These lovely little creatures were quite healthy, if not a bit shy, but swam like Olympic veterans.

It turned out that we needed to return to the shop shortly afterwards to stock up on live food. The shopkeeper informed us that he had restocked his supply of terrapins because they were selling very well. As we chatted he guided us to a large fish tank where he picked up one of the terrapins stating that this particular one wasn't fit for sale. He asked us if we wanted it but the only trouble was he (the terrapin) was blind.

Ruth looked at this larger terrapin's eyes. They were as white as snow without any sign of an iris or pupil whatsoever, just white blank eyes. We agreed to take on this poorly animal so that we could give him a good loving home.

It occurred to me that this would be an ideal opportunity to practise my healing techniques. I wasn't sure if it was possible for him to regain his lost eyesight, but intuitively I felt a positive urge that even some sight was better than none at all. We took him home and settled him into our indoor pond with the other two terrapins.

I didn't waste any time and set about by laying my hands on his shell then gave him prayer through my thoughts. At night time I would repeat this sequence but I also linked up with the healing spirit for just a few minutes each time.

Within a few days my partner excitedly told me that his one eye had returned to almost normal. At least now he could see through his one eye. I thought this was marvellous news but still wondered if the healing that I prayed for really did work.

It came as an amazing surprise that within a few more days our terrapin had regained the use of his other eye. A beautiful, bright iris had appeared where whiteness had once enveloped the vision. Well, if there were any doubts in my mind there certainly aren't any more.

I am confident and can certainly confirm that spiritual healing works with all creatures, whether they be man or beast. I feel truly uplifted by the wondrous powers that God gives so freely.

Ruth was overjoyed and she couldn't wait to spread the news to friends and relatives. Most of them commented that this must have been some sort of miracle. Yes, I thought, many miracles happen every day through spiritual healing.

13th October 2009

While at a healing session I became aware of a spirit standing in between Christine and myself. He seemed to have his hands on both our shoulders. At the time we were sharing a patient which isn't unusual when there are slack periods, it just means that the patient gets two healers for the price of one. As I was about to attune myself I asked the spirit to stand slightly back so that he didn't interfere or disturb us while we were in attunement. I certainly had no objection to him being there.

Generally, if anything like this happens I will push them out of my mind so that I can attune properly with the healing spirit. I couldn't understand the motives of this spirit and I did wonder why he had come in the first place.

For some reason I got the distinct impression that he wanted to help with the healing, but I had trouble in believing that he could, considering the point that the administering spirit would soon be linked up by my colleague and myself. I knew that he was only trying to help in some way, but it was even more strange for me to realise that he precipitated an unusual energy of his own. It gave me thought that perhaps he used to be a spiritual healer when he was on this Earth.

This was a distinct new scenario for me the like of which I have never encountered before. It felt weird as his energies mingled with those of my own and my colleagues.

Since I knew that the main energies came from our administering spirit I had no real problem. When the healing session came to an end our friendly spirit made it known to me that we had met before in this very room where I was situated. He quickly disappeared at that point so I could ask him no further questions. However, I did manage to see his clothing before he disappeared.

I would describe him as wearing a black suit with a light-coloured shirt and a dark cape around his shoulders which reminded me of Victorian days. Perhaps this was a clue for the time period that he was on this Earth plain. It seemed to be a logical explanation.

Once we had finished the healing session with our patient and he retired to the tearoom, I asked my colleague to stay for a moment because I needed to ask her if she had picked up on this gentleman. To my surprise she told me that she had seen him dressed in a suit wearing a cape and that he stood between us. She explained to me that she wasn't sure whether it was her imagination or not. I assured her that what she had witnessed was perfectly correct. She seemed quite thrilled at this outcome which to me only verified what I had witnessed.

It occurred to me that this event must be more exceptional for her considering what I had told her the week before.

I reminded her of the events that happened last week when I had completed the night's healing work and sat on my own, meditating like I usually do.

It was then that I attained inspiration concerning my colleague, Chris, that the spirit world needed her to realise that her senses would increase throughout time. She would become more intuitive while gaining a greater sense of clairvoyance which was already present within her.

This spiritual affirmation would come a lot sooner than she could possibly imagine. It would bring about a new chapter in her life.

She accepted all of this information with great happiness, thanking me for passing on the message. I'm not sure who was more thrilled, but I know it has given me a wonderful privilege to have received such a rare but beautiful message.

17th November 2009

When I have a few minutes break in between healing I often meditate. This particular experience is one of the most beautifully inspirational experiences that I have ever encountered.

As I sat meditating I suddenly found myself being drawn upwards as if I had left my physical body. This gave me a sense of weightlessness. Before I had realised what was going on I found myself floating peacefully into space. I felt as if I wanted to get into the higher realms which I could find in space time. It's a place that is inconceivable and incomprehensible to most people.

My journey began to increase in speed with hundreds of planets of all descriptions slowly coming and going past me. The phenomenal speed increased to a velocity of inconceivable proportions.

This speed caused the many planets to have the effect of blurring into one giant intertwining mass. Colours became vividly complex
and could only be described as a vortex of beautiful flowing colour. As I travelled I felt warm, loved and at perfect peace with myself and my surroundings. The swirling colours started to get brighter as I neared the end where I could see a pure white light that emanated into my comforting vortex of colour. I soon found myself within this spiritual entity of light which drew me further into its magnificence.

As I continued floating downwards there seemed to be a mist of exceptional brilliance which had an ambience of beautiful, peaceful loving that I couldn't escape from, not that I wanted to anyway.

I soon noticed many spiritual beings who had such lovely auras of immense vitality, yet their whole entity seemed as one.

I settled into the middle of these spirits who I recognised instantly as members of my past family. My immediate family sat on chairs within a circle, while past ancestors and friends gathered around them.

How wonderful it was to see my grandmothers and grandfathers along with my closer family. Communication of love seemed to come from all directions with these spirit people each taking turns to express their own thoughts of pure godliness upon me. To hear and reply to each of these wonderful relatives seemed to give me so much wisdom and knowledge that I thought I had been there for hours, yet this turned out to be an impossible timescale for a mortal.

For some reason I became aware that I needed to move on. It felt as though my nan told me that I needed to see and experience more of this amazing world. She turned out to be correct because suddenly I had appeared at the base of the biggest most beautiful tree that would dwarf even the largest on Earth. The tree's leaves were as large as a small car with the different colours of a brilliant rainbow.

Birds also fluttered around this fruiting tree displaying their own method of love. They were inconceivable to our minds, yet their unimaginable colourful form gave such graceful presence that it was hard to be drawn away from them.

I noticed many spirit people, some singing like angels of the highest order, moving around without any fears of anything.

I then found myself floating downwards, underneath the very tree I had stood under mere seconds ago. I could clearly see a massive root structure with worms, moles and insects that I didn't recognise. These creatures were in a harmonious peace with each other with no sign of what we would recognise as a natural food chain linkage. How I marvelled at this space, yet to my mind the area appeared solid in structure.

Down and down I floated until I came into contact with solid rock. I knew that it was the solid rock of Earth but I still wondered how something as solid as rock could be broken down to its anatomical yet transparent form.

I had somehow become aware of how rock is made up of an infinite number of atoms that could so easily move around.

The natural laws of space and time felt prevalent all around me as my thoughts became embedded within this sphere of time.

I continued downwards to find myself going through rivers of water, gas and oil. These were more like oceans in themselves as I tried to find a beginning and an end, but there was none.

I soon came upon the fiery world of molten rock, with flames dancing joyously around my body. They tickled my toes gently while never burning any part of me.

Then there appeared a sphere of blackness drawing closer towards me and I knew that it was the very core of our Earth, with beautiful strong magnetic fields emanating from either ends of this gravitational mass.

It seemed as if there were a pillar of radiating light extruding from either end of the black mass, although it could have been the thousands of travelling waves of magnetism that caused this effect.

How weird it became when I found myself being a part of this incredible process. It felt as though I had become a travelling wave myself, moving upwards in an ever-expanding sequence of energy.

Whilst within this glorious phenomenon that reached for the heavenly sky a voice arose from its depths of tranquillity.

I realised that one of my colleagues was gently talking to me to inform me that another patient was ready for me. I quickly brought myself out of this wonderful meditation with a glow of warm compassion.

Heart Chaos, 3rd February 2011

Having a heart attack isn't something I would recommend, but it is very common in today's society where saturated fats in junk food is perhaps our worst enemy. I have the experience now to talk of it, not only as a physical being but also on the psychic scale.

Thursday 3rd February 2011

I took the dog for a walk as usual but noticed a small but sharp pain in the middle of my chest. At first I thought the cold air that I was breathing in was having an effect on my lungs. Later on however the same thing happened when I had to go across the common with Ted my dog and Michael my son to meet Katie my daughter on her fourteenth birthday.

Once again the pain came but still I was convinced that it was due to the very cold wind getting into my lungs. When I got home from the common I sat down and waited for the now retreating pains to cease altogether. It wasn't long before the pains went but after about half an hour they started to return with a vengeance. I convinced myself that it was nothing more than wind trapped in my lungs so took the appropriate action of using 'Gaviscon' medication.

Of course this didn't make any difference whatsoever but to make things worse both Ruth (my partner) and Michael (my son) had now gone out leaving me on my own.

This particular evening was development night with a group of thirteen people, all of which wanted to further develop their mediumistic abilities in a spiritual manner.

I continued to work on despite the ever-increasing pain in my chest. I had already got the chairs, table and other materials ready. At this point I felt clammy, was perspiring profusely and had to go outside to cool down. I felt some stiffness around my jaw, rather an ache than a pain around the jaw's hinged section. The pain in the chest seemed to be getting tighter which had an effect on my breathing, so I came back indoors and sat down.

A knock on the door soon had me up and Chris our medium came in. We sat for a little while as he told me of his back pain that he was suffering from. I sympathised with him but my own pain soon had me making my excuses to Chris as I quickly took myself upstairs to the bathroom, but my left arm felt very strange indeed.

I was physically sick and felt as if my whole body was out of control and needed to raise the alarm very quickly. Coming out of the bathroom I felt my legs going from under me, my head was spinning and I knew that I couldn't get down the stairs even if I wanted to. I shouted for my sister Emma who had just come in. Woefully I made my way into my bedroom where I collapsed onto the bed.

I can't say whether I was conscious or not but I do remember seeing something which I cannot explain properly.

Three distinct shapes which could have been energy but likened to a curious shape as elongated bright white entities going around my body very fast.

These angel-like entities were seemingly trying to balance my aura field in some strange way. It was very odd as I could clearly see electrically charged spikes of varying colours shooting out from different points around my body.

'Oh my God,' Emma said as she entered my room, 'what has happened to you? You look so grey. I've never seen you like this before! Hang on, Pete, I'll get Mandy. She's done a first aid course.'

It seemed as if several people had come into the room within a few minutes, but I was aware of Justine sat next to me giving comfort just like the bright ones were. How strange this whole scenario felt as I assumed the worst outcome of what was about to happen. I felt that all of this was the precursor to losing my physical body, yet it was at that very point that it all became even stranger. The bright ones who were flying about me suddenly stopped and just looked at me with a quizzical but warm expression about them. A voice came into my mind saying,

'No, not yet, it is too early!'

Well say no more, I thought. I couldn't help but think that all of this was just some sort of nightmare, a dream maybe.

It's true that my mind feels too busy for its own good but is all of this really happening or am I in some sort of illusionary response caused by the turmoil of my body and mind?

One thing is for sure as far as the 'bright ones'

were concerned, they helped me move into a foetal position where I started to pant (hyperventilate). I feel that this was quite necessary from my body's point of view since more air is required to oxygenate the blood and keep the heart pumping. It's even weirder that my thoughts are telling me to do this in the first place, but hey, who am I to argue?

To be honest though it feels only a matter of time

before I black out anyway.

Suddenly, new voices of the 'human variety' distract my thoughts.

'Hello, Peter, I'm a paramedic, soon have you fixed up!' quoted the paramedic and assistant.

Well, that's comforting I thought, but sticking needles into my wrists perhaps isn't.

He tells me that he has given me morphine but asks if I can hold my arm up. Stupid question I thought.

As my right arm began to rise, 'No, the left arm,' said the stranger. I tried to raise my left arm but found it to be rather tingly and almost paralysed.

Yes, those silly thoughts start to emerge, don't they?

Which bit dies next?

My leg maybe? Anyway, the fact that I looked very grey, was perspiring, had no control over my left arm, and my chest was pulling so hard that I thought my heart would just jump out of my body, I certainly felt rough!

I realised that a paramedic had hooked me up to a heart monitor and was checking all of the vital life signs. He then produced a small canister of spray medication which went under my tongue. 'You will be off to hospital soon, Peter,' he told me. 'Don't worry, they're waiting for you in the ops room.'

Very soon I was being taken down the stairs on an ambulance chair then deposited safely inside the ambulance.

I can't say that I enjoyed the ride in this fast vehicle with its blue lights and sirens going because I kept sliding down the bed, thinking that I was going to fall out of the back doors. Ambulances are not built for comfort.

More morphine was administered but it made little impact on the hellish pain I was going through.

However, on a psychic sense I could feel a deep warm love, an acceptance of the circumstances and the wonderful knowledge that a special spirit was next to me, comforting my very thoughts. I noticed that my aura field around my entire presence lacked the usual bright cheerful colours, replaced by those of a greyish dull shade that produced a negative state and high electrical discharges, much like a battery that is in short circuit mode due to damage.

We arrived at the hospital but I never realised that the back doors of the ambulance had been opened. I must have passed out at that particular time or perhaps my heart had stopped? The next thing that I can remember was when I was being wheeled towards the ops room where I noticed Ruth, Tina her sister and Dawn my daughter who were all sitting by some doors.

I wondered how they actually beat me to the hospital since I had been taken there very quickly. Time had obviously passed me by although the last thing I can remember were the doors of the ambulance opening. From then on I must have blacked out or actually died!

I can only assume that once at the hospital the rapid response team had gone into overdrive very quickly indeed.

I must have been in the resuscitation room and then moved quickly to the procedure room where the surgeon and his team were waiting. They all had a specific job to do and answered to the surgeon's voice like remote control. I can only describe this set up as truly wonderful clockwork precision.

As I lay there I looked straight towards the ceiling.

To my surprise it appeared as if I was being watched by many ancient Chinese gentlemen who took great interest in what was going on below them. I can only describe this setting as a type of amphitheatre for medical doctors or surgeons.

Although Mr Smith the surgeon in charge of me had no idea of what I could see on a psychic nature, they would have had kittens if they had indeed witnessed what I saw. There were at least six spirit surgeons watching and pondering over Mr Smith's skills.

Two prominent Chinese surgeons stood out of the pack. One had a drooping moustache and a round type of headwear. The other wore similar clothing as he wandered off to look at what instruments were on the trolley to the right of me.

Names such as Chung Meng Yin and Yeng appeared in my mind who seemed to be inspiring Mr Smith in the ways that best suited my chances of survival. Other spirit surgeons wandered around watching the rest of the team, but one in particular wasn't happy with a certain piece of equipment. In fact, he removed two pieces of wire from a table, although I couldn't tell you what they would be used for.

The procedure got underway but I just lay there quite still and without any fear whatsoever. Now that I knew I was in the very best of company there was very little to worry about.

The scenario reminded me of when one is at a theatre with spirits looking on from balcony seats encompassing the whole scenario or perhaps the final scene of the drama.

Mr Smith seemed to be in full flow and had a superior confidence that shone out to his team members. Mr Smith pondered for a few seconds on a length of wire when the Chinese spirit said, 'No, not that one, man, the other one.' This was in reply to the physical surgeon questioning whether to use the thinner wire that would go up through my arm to the artery or the thicker one. When Mr Smith (surgeon) said, 'No, we'll use the other one,' the spirit surgeon replied, 'That's right, now you have got the idea.'

All went very well and the routine operation was finally completed.

Mr Smith then left with most of his team, although I did overhear one nurse say to the other nurse, 'Where's it gone?' They must have found whatever they were looking for because they did not stay very long afterwards.

Peace at last has settled down upon my body, the drama was done, but the involvement of both the physical body and psychic experience will stay in my mind for a very long time indeed.

This paradoxical setting over and done with, I was taken to my recovery room where I stayed for five weeks. I had my computer brought in and wrote these notes up while I was sat in recovery.

3rd November 2018

It was at a slack time before the healing session had begun that I sat quietly on my own meditating. I had the impression that a spirit was close by so I asked him to come closer to me. To my surprise he granted my request.

There he was. He seemed to be quite tall and muscular with a peaceful yet spiritual manner. Quite honestly I jumped a little because I could feel his strong inspirational spiritual energies. Smiling broadly, I introduced myself.

He made it known to me that he knew who I was.

It's strange how he vanished at that point but not before I had thanked him for his presence.

I didn't get the chance to find out who he was or even

what he was doing there, but that really doesn't matter to me because I felt privileged to have met him. I felt very humbled to have had this wonderful experience which made my day.

A Mystical Life

Part 2

This section deals with the experiences of more healing sessions and the divine service which takes place on a Sunday evening. Spirits usually have a habit of turning up just about anywhere, so my own home holds no prohibition to them and are included here.

Chapter 7

Healing
16th March 2010

When I first entered the healing room in my capacity of a healing medium I perceived the presence of a spirit. Taking little notice of this phenomena I quickly attuned myself in readiness for my first patient. After the healing came to its natural conclusion, I could clearly hear the visiting spirit moving around from chair to chair from the back of the room down to where the rest of the healing session was taking place. Commenting to my colleague Christine who had doubled up with me that a presence was around us, she listened for the spirit's movements. There were only a few patients that evening so we had finished earlier than usual. I spoke to the spirit who revealed his name as Michael Granger.

I asked him if he used to be a member of the church but he replied with an emphatic no. I then proceeded to ask him if he had lived within the grounds before the church was built. He told me that he had. He gave me an image of an old Victorian house which could have been on the grounds when he was alive. I told him not to interfere with any of the healers when work was going on but, quite frankly, he seemed content to just move around away from the healers.

When all was quiet we sat with some of our colleagues chatting about the spirit's presence. Our healing leader was standing at the old white grand piano when suddenly she shouted out.

'Oh my God, something just walked past me. It was a spirit, I saw it!'

I told her that the spirit had been here all night and told

her the information that I had learnt. She proceeded to pick up a plate

from the small white coloured grand piano which promptly shattered in her hand, causing her to drop it on the floor.

The noise echoed around the room as she shouted out.

'He pulled it out of my hand! I didn't do anything except pick the plate up!'

We asked her if she was alright. She nodded and with a smile she calmly went to get a dustpan and brush to sweep up the pieces of broken crockery.

My attention had turned to listening for voices of other spirit activity. There were definitely two female spirits present who were quietly humming to the sound of the meditation music. They started to chatter in a coherent manner although it was a bit too quiet for me to make out exactly what they were saying. I did have the impression that they were talking about the male spirit who had frightened the life out of our healing leader.

We settled back down to give healing to the last of our colleagues. Shortly after we had finished one of our female healing mediums told me that the male spirit had been quite noisy when moving around the chairs, and that he had come right down to the side where we sat. I agreed with this account that he had been quite noisy and added that his character had suggested to me that he was a bit of a rogue in his time on Earth. It occurred to me that nothing has changed. I don't feel that we have seen the last of incarnate spirit Michael Granger.

6th June 2010

During this evening's divine service, Patricia R (name withheld) took to the platform to give out messages from a spirit to the congregation. I sat and listened with interest as she demonstrated her mediumship skills. I soon started to note that symbols were being shown to me through my psychic senses. The first symbol came as a letter D which I presumed was the initial of a name. I then saw three white eggs in a row. I did think that there could well have been faces drawn on their surface but there were no details of a face on any of them. Lastly, I received the impression of a canvas of white colour which I thought must be quite significant to her. Surprisingly, I also saw a picture of a child on a tricycle, happy as could be. This is probably a memory linked to earlier times.

I pondered on these strange symbols for only a few moments but realised that I would have to tell the medium about them, because when I start receiving symbols when sat close to the platform I know that a message is being relayed to me for the working medium.

When the service ended I went into the tearoom with my family and had a refreshing cup of tea. I thought that the tea was quite good but considering the medium had told the tea maker that she makes rubbish tea, especially after the fact that the medium had given her a spirit message, was perhaps not what this young lady needed to hear.

After I had finished my tea I decided to go and talk to Patricia. She was quite pleased to see me and even more pleased when I said that I had a message for her. She said that I always gave her messages when she visited us and that I was the only one to do that, so thanked me. I quietly proceeded to tell her what I had seen and she was quite surprised at what I told her. She commented that the colour white was very significant because her former name had been White. The three white eggs symbolised Easter when she had lost her son David (D). The tricycle had belonged to David who used to love playing on it.

She thanked me for being so accurate but it pleased me even more that everything had made sense to her and I thanked my spirit friends for bringing this message to me for her.

9th June 2010

Even I get a little spooked when spirits decide to show themselves to me. I was lying in bed one night but for some reason I felt a little nervous. I'm not sure why but the atmosphere seemed a bit strange, although maybe it had something to do with the weird noises I could hear whilst listening to my audio tape story. My partner, Ruth, had started to settle down for the night but I knew that I had to turn around to look at her, don't ask me why, senses are like that, aren't they?

I nearly always go with my senses. I saw three or maybe four spirits standing right at the side of where she lay. The darkened silhouettes were quite distinct and in the shape of a human spirit form, but no details could be identified although they appeared as the human male. Instinctively, I put my outstretched hand, palm up, and told the spirits to stand back just in case Ruth happened to turn around and see them. I used telepathy as my mode of communication. Ruth asked me what I was doing so I just said, 'Nothing, dear, go to sleep.' Luckily, she did, I didn't want her to be frightened.

It startled me to be quite frank, but whoever they were they soon vanished and I returned to my audio tape story not thinking any more about this strange event.

It's a pity that these spirits didn't come and stand by me because then I wouldn't have been so startled and I would certainly have tried to find out who they were and what they wanted.

11th June 2010

It was very strange how this particular evening worked out because I was supposed to be going to my local club with Ruth, but unfortunately it had been cancelled.

My sister Emma had told me about a new spiritualist

church that had opened about a year ago. She had asked me to go with her and Penny, my other sister, so I thought that this might be an opportune time to visit the establishment.

The church was a pleasant one and the people were friendly. I really didn't expect too much to happen but when the service started I noticed a young spirit black girl walk in front of where I sat. She had a beautiful white dress on which reminded me of weddings. She could only have been about nine years old but she seemed happy enough. I whispered to Emma that I had just witnessed a young spirit girl in front of us and told her that I would speak about it when the service had ended.

The young girl stayed around us for most of the night but she made sure that I knew that she was there as she kept touching my knee with her lovely slender hands. I smiled at her and assured her that I could see her quite plainly. She seemed to like this fact and tried to tell me her name. I must admit I struggled with this because I couldn't quite make it out. It seemed to be something like 'Cil' or 'Syl'. I discounted 'Cin' for Cindy because it sounded like Cynthia, but I knew that it wasn't this as it sounded more like Sil. I left this alone not wanting to ponder upon it too much as it would only confuse me even more. I tried to work out some facts about this child but it soon occurred to me that she was not one for many words. Her actions though suggested that she was a cuddly type of person, one who would just come up to you and show her warmth with a loving squeeze or maybe stroke the person's face.

The little girl seemed to be around Emma quite a lot, and since I couldn't see any other connection I assumed that it was somehow meant for her or somebody close to her. How stupid, I thought to myself, it must be connected to Rob, Emma's husband, who is probably of Caribbean origin or ancestry. Since I saw pictures that depicted the warm glow of islands in the ocean, I believed that I must be on the right track. I could not see the relationship between Rob and this child, so I thought it best if I asked him when we next met.

Speaking to Emma after the service had finished, I tried once again to come up with a name for my spirit messenger. I'm glad to say that when I gave the first three letters 'Syl', Emma told me that I was almost there. It was Silvia and she was Rob's mother! I said that I didn't understand how a nine year old girl could possibly be Rob's mother, but she told me that it was Rob who was nine years old when his mother died. My God, I thought, so that's the connection with Rob.

It is important at this stage to point out that spirits can show themselves in a form that suggests other clues. This happened here with the age connected with Rob at the time of her transition. Those young days must have been very happy ones for her as it showed with the lovely smile she portrayed on her face.

I asked Emma about the beautiful bell-shaped white dress that she wore, because usually there is a significant point attached to something so unusual. Emma immediately stated that Rob has a framed photograph of his mum in her wedding dress and she appeared to be very happy. This was an amazing way to show me the relationship.

It turns out that the actual shape of the dress did not really matter, just the actual significance of it being a wedding dress and the relationship between mother and son.

When I eventually spoke to Rob he confirmed that his mother certainly was the sort of person who would just come up to you and give you a cuddle without many words being spoken. He told me that she took much in but spoke little. It was her nature. I told him that the only message that I could relay to him was that his mum is around him, loves him very much and that she is happy where she is. There seemed little else I could give to Rob, but I knew it was enough because he told me that I was the first person to ever do what I had just done. Well, that's just beautiful, isn't it?

4th September 2010

I was talking to Liz (a medium) outside our church - Kings Heath spiritualist. I mentioned that mediums didn't get messages very often and she concurred with what I said. I observed that
sometimes I did see or feel the spirit presence on the platform. If this occurred I would then relay any message to her afterwards.

The service got underway and eventually Liz came on to deliver her demonstration of mediumship. It must have been about halfway through her delivery when I noticed the presence of a spirit around me. The spirit decided to give me a name, Mahonia, which I knew was the name of a flowering shrub. There are two varieties which I knew were Mahonia Aquilegia and Mahonia Veronica, with both producing white or violet flowers.

Curiously, I felt a terrible pain in my head which seemed to be more on the one side. This travelled down the left side of my neck and continued down the same side of my body. I asked the spirit to take the pain away since I had realised that this spirit had suffered the same trauma just before death. I knew the spirit was male but he impressed upon me that he was looking after Liz and that he loved her very much. He was obviously very close to her and seemed to be a fatherlike figure to her.

It was at this point that I started to cough quite badly; this was unusual for me to say the least. It actually felt as if I had smoked a dozen cigarettes all at once and I felt as if I was choking. This was surely the spirit giving me more information but I do wish that they would give me a little more notice of their intentions because it can really catch you off guard. I also bizarrely saw an ironing board along with a wooden stool, although I didn't know what these items meant.

I passed on the message to Liz and to my surprise she told me that it must have been her dear old dad. Apparently, he had been a very keen gardener who would have known these varieties of plants, and that he had suffered a stroke down the left side of his body which took his life.

She laughed when she noticed how badly I started to cough but said that it was exactly what her dad would have done due to his heavy smoking habit.

The ironing board came as no surprise to her because she stated that she had a lot of ironing to do but kept putting it off. She couldn't quite understand the significance of the stool, so I reminded her of the funny story that she had used in her deliverance. She smiled when she realised that it was the same connection. To explain briefly, she had used a small stool to climb on and promptly fell off it. I must point out that the appearance of these two objects had already come to light to me before the story was told on the platform.

She was very content with my message especially with the plant names I gave. The stroke her father had suffered had never been mentioned by any other medium so came as a surprise. My message to her gave her some comfort.

24th October 2010

A peculiar evening occurred while I sat within the divine service at our spiritualist church. As the service got underway, I became aware of what I thought was a person trying to come around myself and Teddy my guide dog. I quickly put my hand out to stop this person from tripping over Teddy when I realised that the person turned out to be a spirit. I smiled at this and hoped nobody had seen me put my hand out. When the medium (Terry C) started his deliverance, he must have seen my reaction because he commented, 'Looks like the spirits have already arrived, my friends.' The service went very well, even if a spirit was present but not around me.

At home that night when I retired to bed a voice called out my name and at the same time the bedside table lamp came on. The voice was that of a female, but I could also sense the presence of a spirit within the bedroom. I turned out the lamp thanking the spirit for its presence. I started to settle down with my audiobook but I could not understand why it appeared so light again in the room until I checked whether the lamp had come back on or not. It had, but it seemed as if somebody was trying to tell me something. I quickly attuned myself to that of the spirit whereupon I realised the name Elizabeth. She was trying to make me aware of my mother and that I should telephone her the next morning. Automatically I considered that she was in some sort of trouble, but Elizabeth seemed to assure me that all was well.

How strange I thought. I wondered if my mom had seen a spirit or maybe felt the presence of one which could have frightened her. I telephoned her the next day and asked her if she was alright. She said that she was but had taken a tumble last night hurting her neck.

She proceeded to tell me that she had taken some paracetamol and returned to bed where the pain subsided.

'How did you know?' Mom enquired.

'Well,' I said, 'Elizabeth made me aware that something was not quite right.'

I told her the full story and she was amazed.

'It looks like you're being looked after quite well by the spirits, aren't you?'

'They must be looking after you as well,' I replied with

a wry smile.

To verify who Elizabeth was within the family, I asked Mom if she knew this lady.

'Oh yes, it must be Beth. She was my grandmother's sister, my great aunt. How strange that she should come around.'

I told Mom that many spirits are looking after her and that I had received communication with this spirit lady in the past.

2nd November 2010

While in a quiet spell where I just sit and meditate during the healing session, I could clearly hear movement next to a stack of chairs at the far end of the room. There was only one patient receiving healing by our healing leader so I kept quiet so as not to disturb them. Shortly afterwards I heard loud footsteps moving quickly towards me. I knew that no other physical being was present. Suddenly this presence was behind me.

My chair vibrated violently for a few seconds then stopped. I turned my head and moved my hands slightly to check for a physical presence but nothing was there. Then I went bitterly cold down my right side which made me shiver. I spoke through my mind to this mischievous spirit telling him that I was a child of God and that he could not scare me. I then told him to go back to where he came from and not to interfere with any of the patients during healing. The coldness ceased abruptly and all went quiet. I guess I knew who this spirit was because I recognised his vibrations as the one I know as Michael Granger.

At that point when our healing leader had completed her healing session one of my colleagues came to fetch me saying that there were no more patients. I told her what went on once we had come into the foyer which made her shiver a little. Julie overheard what I had experienced and told us that she had been pulled by the arm by the same entity. She also said that she didn't think he was malicious but rather mischievous in character. I agreed with her but it's quite strange that only the two of us were picking up on this spirit as we both knew that he visited us quite regularly. I suppose we are more sensitive to the presence of spirits but I would love to know his history and why he appears while healing is taking place.

16th January 2011

I've come across some strange energies throughout my life including those of spirits at different levels, but the energy force that I encountered this particular evening while at the divine service at our church surpassed all other previous experiences. The service had just got underway with the first song of the evening when suddenly a force of strong energy passed in front of me. To actually try and explain this force is quite difficult, but if one imagines a field of electromagnetic power then perhaps you may understand how powerful it actually felt. As it occurred I followed the movement of this strange energy with my paranormal vision which is the same as seeing a spirit, otherwise known as the third eye, and got another shock when I went completely dizzy. The dizziness only lasted for a couple of seconds but the effect that it had on me felt quite overwhelming.

My God, I thought, what the hell was that?

It certainly wasn't the energy of a ghost, spirit or higher entity as I know these types of energy patterns from my past experiences. I normally feel or sense the presence of these.

I could only assume that in some weird way this energy must be that of a magnetic force field. There was no other explanation that I could logically explain this type of phenomena. Previous experiences have shown wonderful, gentle, serene forces. This didn't seem to make much sense at all.

I pondered for some thirty minutes but my intuition only gave me a sense of illness somewhere around me. I discounted my sister Emma who was sat two chairs away from me as her energies didn't seem to match those that I encountered, yet I knew that it must be someone quite close by.

At the end of a lovely service I spoke to a well recognised medium, Ralph, and told him about my experience. I explained that I thought it must be some type of illness as this was the only explanation I could give at the time. He seemed surprised by what I told him, but his own reply certainly made me think.

'I know that you can't see, Peter, nor could you realise what has just taken place. The lady who was sitting in front of you had a very distressing time, her emotions were very high and she was crying profusely. The medium that was on the stage, upon observing what was happening, came down and put her arms around her in a comforting way. This lady abruptly got up and left the building very quickly.'

At this juncture my sister Emma came over and informed me she was going straight home as she felt very poorly. As she left my mother, who was sat by my side, informed me that Emma had almost fainted twice with the pain she was suffering and had to sit down on two occasions during the service's songs.

Well, to say that I was gobsmacked would be an understatement. Maybe this is the reason why I felt this strange yet very powerful phenomena. It was most interesting though, because I can usually sense illness but never on a scale such as this. Generally, I pick up on the pain of a person which then goes away. I have to wonder if the spirit world is trying to show me something new to my senses but a lot more powerful in context. It did show me however that we know very little of real phenomena, its effects and causes.

(Please refer to chapter - Heart Attack, 3rd February 2011 to understand this sort of phenomena)

24th March 2011
Home Circle
A home circle is a meeting of a group of like-minded people who seek to develop their psychic and mediumistic skills.

At this week's home circle it was decided to restructure part of the way that we run the meeting. Chris suggested that a half hour session of complete silence might help the students develop their skills. I thought that this was a good idea but moreover it would serve to bring the spirits closer to us all.

We had previously discussed the phenomena of physical mediumship, something which I have personally always wanted to do.

The usual meditation went very well and then came the point to try our silence routine. At first it seemed quiet but I soon recognised that energies were being formed above the heads of the students. I noticed three orbs moving about, and to my surprise the figure of a male spirit became clearly visible. This spirit was very tall, at least six feet five. He appeared to be wearing a brown jacket with matching trousers. He was quite thin in stature and in his late fifties or early sixties. Silently he bent down where one of the students, Adrian, sat then quickly disappeared.

Moments later another spirit appeared but this time it was in the form of a crouched older lady who simply walked about two steps and then disappeared. I would have put her in her fifties. The only other energy I noticed was that of a more 'pure energy' which floated in one corner of the room near the ceiling. I felt that this was a fantastic experience and couldn't wait to hear if any of the other students had witnessed the same phenomena.

Unsurprisingly, Mandy had also seen what I had observed. I asked the rest of the group if they had witnessed anything but alas nobody had. If this was only the start then I hold great expectations for the future.

28th December 2013

This evening when I retired to bed all seemed to be calm and tranquil. At about one o'clock I was awoken to feel the presence of a spirit around me. Suddenly, I distinctly heard the sound of fingers running across the top of the grid of the radiator in our bedroom.

If one could imagine the nail of a finger running across the radiator then one can easily imagine the sound it makes. The radiator is only about five or six feet from my bed so I turned my head towards the sound in an automatic response. I told the intruding spirit that it was a good trick but to leave me alone to rest in peace. This he did but it still unsettled me somewhat.

30th December 2013

As I went to bed this evening the sound of the nails on the radiator two evenings earlier was still on my mind, although it had not perturbed me too much. At around two o'clock I was awoken from my sleep once again. The atmosphere felt unsettled and as I lay still in my bed I heard a strange noise. If one could imagine turning on a hosepipe full blast at a window then this is how it sounded to me. I could hear the water pounding on the glass then running off down onto the ground from the windowsill. I was by any standards of consciousness wide awake and fully aware of what I was hearing. It puzzled me how this could possibly occur, but there again it appears that spirits can conjure up anything that they please in a psychic manner. I did wonder however whether this could be the work of a mischievous spirit or one that may have been trying to get my attention. Whatever the reason, it certainly drew my attention to the spirit!

31st December 2013

I'm not sure what I expected this particular night when I finally went to bed after celebrating the new year. In fact, I was in quite a jolly mood and fell straight to sleep. I awoke at five o'clock in the morning thinking how peaceful and quiet it was.

Turning over I became aware that the bathroom shower switch was being turned on and off. I automatically touched my wife Helen to make sure she was in bed just in case she had gone to the bathroom, but she lay beside me fast asleep.

The switch is a pull cord and the bathroom is directly behind the wall where the bed was positioned. The cord was pulled I would estimate at least around ten to twelve times. As I arose to investigate the sound it stopped as suddenly as it had started.

This displeased me somewhat and I even sent a prayer out to this annoying spirit to stop its antics or come talk to me in person. All became calm and I went back to sleep after about half an hour.

2nd November 2014

I always enjoy the Sunday divine service but on this particular day it was slightly unusual. A lady had spoken to our healing leader to ask if it were possible to have some spiritual healing. She was redirected to myself since there was time before the service got underway. Her name was Sue and although I did not recognise her I simply asked her to sit next to me. She told me that she had a seven centimetre hole in her stomach but didn't explain how and why it was there.

I explained to her how spiritual healing works and that it would be done through me holding onto her hands so that contact could be maintained. Without hesitation I got on with the healing. When the healing came to an end Sue told me how exhilarated and refreshed she felt. She commented that she now had no pain anymore and a feeling of complete joy had overwhelmed her. She thanked me and went off to her seat.

A couple of weeks later she returned and told me that she had been given a scan on her stomach and that the doctors had been baffled at what they saw.

The hole had shrunk from seven centimetres down to three. They couldn't understand why this had happened after the length of time the hole had been there.

She thanked me profusely but I said no thanks were required since it was a spirit who had intervened to help her. I was only the vessel of their energy and that I was glad to be of some service to them and her and anybody who needed healing.

Seeing spirits is nothing unusual for my senses since I have been seeing them since I was four years old. Sometimes I see them as any other human would see another human even though I am blind.

Other times I see them as silhouettes, yet I know what they are wearing, their personality, their relationship to a person and even when they were holding something.

The following are two examples of what I have experienced during our divine service:

7th November 2014

Chris and Pat S were the speaker and medium at the divine service. Chris gave an illuminating speech as my third eye roamed the platform area. I soon noticed the distinct shape of a spirit monk who walked slowly onto the platform to stand close to Chris. My senses told me that he was from the sixteenth century. He was holding a Bible and wearing a habit which could possibly have been made from sackcloth which was darkish cream in colour.

This hooded monk was not a relation of the family nor genetically linked, yet he resembled himself to be some sort of spirit helper towards Chris. Relaying this information to Chris after the service came as no surprise to him as he told me that others have also advised him of this monk's presence before.

30th November 2014

At the divine service the medium, Lorraine G, and her husband Ian (speaker), were on the platform. When Ian came on to deliver his philosophical speech I couldn't help but notice that a lady was standing to his right. She only came up to his shoulders in height, was slightly built and wearing a blue dress that finished just below her knees. It occurred to me that she was his mother, a pleasant lady, but I knew that she was the type who wouldn't stand for any nonsense.

When Lorraine walked onto the stage I immediately noticed a tall gentleman standing next to her. He appeared to be wearing smart casual wear, yet I could not decide whether he was a relative or a close friend which seemed a little strange to me and I would have to get confirmation from Lorraine herself.

At the same time I noticed an older lady kneeling at the front of the platform, very obviously in prayer, bending down towards the floor where either a Bible or prayer book lay. This spirit lady also moved her right hand in an upward/downwards gesture as if praying for Lorraine. In my own understanding this spirit lady was without any doubt very committed to the Catholic religion.

After the service had finished I managed to speak to the medium before she went home. She confirmed that the lady by Ian's side was indeed his mother. She also confirmed the tall man but would not go into any detail about him. Following on she confirmed the Catholic lady but could not tell me exactly who she was since she knew many Catholics.

1st February 2015

Once again at the divine service I noticed a spirit appear on the platform. The mediums this evening were my friends Ralph and Sharon.

When Ralph came on to give his philosophy I became aware of something flashing past me very quickly and running up onto the stage. It was a dog! The dog stopped in front of Ralph; it was of medium height and build and very overweight.

The dog then disappeared and the image of a spirit man appeared. This spirit was about the same height as Ralph, well-built and stocky. He may have worn a suit, I couldn't quite see since his back was towards me, but he also wore a heavy overcoat which may have made him look larger than he actually was. I sensed that he was perhaps a relative of Ralph's.

After the service I asked Ralph if I could have a quick word with him. I told him what I had seen and he smiled.

'That was my dog, and yes, he was overfed. As far as the man goes, he was my brother who always wore suits and had a big overcoat.'

15th February 2015

It's amazing to think that whenever I go to my church on a Sunday I look forward to seeing spirits on the platform. This day was no different. The medium Pat S was demonstrating her mediumship.

I've seen many things in my life but never a cow on the platform. No, I'm not referring to the medium! It was the image of a cow who stood directly in front of her. I couldn't help think that if that cow had moved backwards it would cause poor old Pat to suffer an amusing event.

I couldn't quite get its name so I named it Daisy. The animal was a black and white Friesian. It occurred to me that the medium certainly must have some unusual pets. The next thing I saw was a solid oak table that looked quite heavy. I presumed that this must have been a memory link, but still, this was quite an unusual occurrence to say the least.

While there were no more objects I got the name of John linked to the medium herself, but it appeared that this gent had some sort of fantasy with nurses' uniforms. Dare I ask her afterwards?

Once the demonstration was over I asked the medium if she had time for a little chat and explained to her what I had seen. The medium wasn't surprised about what apparently had been her pet cow who she had called Daisy and had lived on her farm. She also remembers the heavy old oak table but blushed when I talked about John who turned out to be her past husband.

'Yes,' she said, 'you picked up on my husband, and yes, he did have a thing about nurses' uniforms, but perhaps we should not go there since it's a bit embarrassing.'

'You're right,' I replied, 'we'll keep quiet about it.'

The way this was going was a bit concerning. What if somebody had a pet elephant? Perhaps it'll be a pink one or maybe Dumbo would come for a visit. The mind boggles.

21st February 2015

I find it quite extraordinary sometimes when spirits come visiting during the early hours of the morning as one did at 2.30am on this particular day. I had awoken and found it quite hard to go back to sleep, mainly due to my sensing a nearby spirit. Somehow I just knew that he was going to creep up on me and try and take me unawares.

Well, that's exactly what he did, yet at the same time my inner voice suddenly stated, 'Something is on my shoulder!' I believe this is proof positive that we all have a soul or spirit within us.

The spirit within my room began to pull the duvet cover down the bed, but since I wasn't asleep I grabbed the cover and pulled it back up to my neck. I then started to look around very carefully for the spirit but to no avail. Perhaps he didn't like the way that I told him to stop being so annoying and to go away. That did the trick. Yet I was not concerned whatsoever about the spirit's presence. However, the peculiarity of the voice of my innermost mind gave me something to think about, as I definitely did not physically speak those words and I was not even thinking them in my conscious mind. Perhaps this voice, which announced itself with a clear distinct vocabulary, was my own 'inner voice' spirit within. Even more curious, this announcement also appeared to be shown to me as a typed written sentence on a strip of paper with an audio voice complementing its presence.

Maybe this type of phenomena is something new to me. It certainly has its uses when trying to establish an alert of danger if that was the case, but it was not since I had become aware of it at least a couple of seconds before the incident. The only other explanation was that it was the same spirit taking the mickey out of me.

24th February 2015

I had another encounter with a spirit this morning at 1.30am. Once again I was having trouble getting to sleep but I soon became aware that a spirit presence was around. I began thinking to myself what sort of antics this spirit would bring me this morning. He didn't take long as all of a sudden I heard a guitar being strummed, followed by another four strokes which may have been either a practice session or simply because this spirit was a bit mischievous.

'That's very clever,' I said, 'now can I get to sleep?'

The spirit disappeared and all went quiet. Just for the record my son, Michael, does have a guitar in his bedroom but he was fast asleep according to the snoring which echoed from his room.

4th April 2015

I attended a healing workshop this afternoon. It concerned 'spirit energy' compared and combined with our own energies. The energy from a spirit is very subtle but is fully noticeable when a 'healing medium' is using it to heal a person. However, when a person uses their 'own energies' along with the 'spirit energy', one can really appreciate the difference it makes.

When my healing partner used 'spirit energy' it felt like a tingling sensation that started from the top of my head until it eventually crept all the way down to the tips of my toes, just before the healing session ended. When she combined her own energies with those of the spirit it took on a more invigorating role.

When the healing tutor said I might struggle a little with this combination of two energies, I do not think she could have been further from the truth. In fact, I use this combination of energies if the patient specifies a particular problem such as anxiety or is unable to settle down during the healing session. It's just a case of extending my energies around the patient like wrapping up a person with an aura but seeing the health issue on a particular part of their body and working with that part.

When we reversed roles my healing partner said that the spirit energy was that of a lovely subtle energy, but when she felt the combination of my own energy she noticed how much stronger in the body the energies were.

Commenting on this she told me how she felt my fingers vibrate as I held her hands and how she felt an overwhelming power that swept through every part of her body, right down to the tips of the toes.

People often say that they feel this vibration through my fingers and hands, yet on this particular occasion I did not feel my own fingers vibrate at all. I have always noticed how energies from spirits affect myself. It can be quite powerful or as subtle as a feather floating on the wind. We have to understand that the passive healer is attuned to the spirits and that responsibility is therefore on the healing medium in this process.

It looked like all of the trainee healers had learnt a great deal. Indeed, I feel my healing partner should do very well with more experience. After the session ended we all sat and chatted for a while.

It was while we were talking that I got the image of three babies sitting in bouncy chairs. One baby was dressed in blue for a boy, one had a pink dummy in her mouth, and the third was dressed in white. I then noticed a stained glass window in the background of many people including a nun dressed in a light blue and white habit.

I asked if any of the trainees had triplets or worked with young children. One of the group suggested that Janet had experience in this field. Hearing her name being mentioned, Janet told me that she used to work with babies in a creche and there had been three babies whose mother had to go to work.

Margaret (tutor) announced that the nun was most likely her spirit guide. This seemed to make sense yet a nagging feeling

came over me about this reading, but I had to go home and accept the situation as it was.

That nagging feeling continued all the way home and it didn't stop until Sunday afternoon. The spirit messenger was determined to show her real value to me.

The picture turned yet again to that of three long tables covered in white linen and people sitting down eating food while listening to a speaker who had stood up to give his speech. Strangely however, on each separate set of tables a speaker stood up. Some of the younger men on one table wore grey suits, like a formal dress code, while the older gents tended to wear black jackets and trousers.

Attending the divine service on this day was Hugh and Margaret D who gave an enlightened service and messages to the audience. After the service had finished I went to the tearoom.

Janet, who was also in attendance at this evening's divine service, came over and sat opposite to where I was sitting.

I told her that there was more to be given to her concerning the babies, and that when I saw the baby in white clothing I believed that this baby and even possibly the other two babies were in Heaven. I didn't think that the baby in white even saw the Earth, mainly because there was no determinable sex to the child.

She proceeded to inform me that she had lost a child before birth and that she didn't know the sex of the baby. The other two babies were indeed in Heaven, one not living long after birth. These were relatives of hers.

Janet continued telling me that there were going to be three weddings this year but did not know whether a formal hat and tail wedding was on the cards. I expect she will let me know when the happy day comes along. I also believe that at least one of the weddings would be in a Catholic church, hence the stained glass window and the nun dressed in her habit. Finally, it had all come together to make a very interesting reading even though it was stretched out by a day.

9th June 2015

There's never a dull moment when a spirit comes calling at our house. My son Michael had gone out for the evening, so it was no surprise to that at 11.10pm I heard keys opening up the front door and then closing it. I even commented to Helen, my wife, that Mike had just come in.

I thought it a little odd though that Mike was making such a noise rattling his keys as he made his way towards the back room where he opened the door, went into the kitchen and started to make more rattling sounds.

All went quiet after a few minutes and I certainly did not hear him go into his bedroom. I soon settled down and thought nothing else about it until the next morning, when in strolled Mike at eleven o'clock. He told me that he had not come home the previous evening since he had stayed at his friend's house.

I can only perceive that the man who entered our house was that of a spirit, yet he knew exactly the layout of this house so it brings me to the conclusion that this spirit may well have been a former resident going into his own house after a night out.

14th June 2015

I woke early this morning to hear somebody going down the stairs. Naturally, I thought it was Mike my son. I couldn't believe my ears when I clearly heard Teddy my guide dog jumping around as if Mike was playing with him.

I got up and went down the stairs into the back room where Teddy sleeps and found him lying there, half asleep. I checked the door to see if Mike was outside having a cigarette as he usually does, but there wasn't a sign of him anywhere and both doors were locked. Once again it looked as if the spirit had returned. I even tried to use my senses to see if he was still there but I could not pick up on any such entity. Oh well, it's nothing strange so I went back to bed. It was weird though because something woke me up again on two further occasions within a few hours and I still could l not focus on anything out of the ordinary. Hmm, there's nothing quite normal in this house as far as the spirit is concerned.

24th July 2015

My mediumship is developing very well when I attend the open circle with Amanda H as circle leader. The psychometry is a great way in development terms, but it can come up with some intriguing results, as I found out last week and today.

Last week saw me give out what I can only describe as emotional turmoil. This type of emotion overcame my senses with not only an emotional force, but actual pressure to the top of my head and a pulsating sensation on my heart. The emotional turmoil pointed to some type of mental disorder, one which somehow carried the characteristics of multiple confusion where there may be more than one individual concerned.

I told the lady to whom it was intended that I felt drained with so much emotion. I said that it must be around this particular lady but not necessarily her condition. That much anxiety was prevalent due to this person's rapid pulsations of the heart. These emotions then left my senses and I was once again free of people's emotions.

The lady told me that she had been struggling with her family where three of them had the condition of autism and that the heart pulsations may have been when anxiety for the three was high, yet it may also have been as a result of the autism in one or two of the others. She openly told the group of sitters how it affected her and how she struggled to cope with the situation.

The circle group were very quiet but much empathy and some helpful information was given from the group and myself.

Strangely enough one person came up to me after the circle closed and asked for healing while I sat in the tearoom having a cuppa. I told her to sit next to me and I promptly gave her some healing. Two others also came to me for advice and a reading. Maybe it was the emotion that brought them forward, but I am always ready to help anybody who asks for my help.

In today's psychometry all seemed quite normal at first, but once again a dark emotion swept over me. It felt as if there was some big secret, a skeleton in the cupboard so to say, yet I could not unlock this dark door. It held me there like a hangman's noose or a pair of gravity boots stuck in a place that was not pleasant.

When it came to me giving this lady my reading all went well with an accurate account of the events that I passed on to her.

I apologised to her because I was not of the intention of knowing her dark secrets if there were any, since this is a personal matter and I had no intention of upsetting her. Besides, it would be unethical for any medium to delve into other people's personal affairs. The fact that after the circle ended another person came up to me and told me that I was not far from the truth just shows how gossiping lends its hand to those of that cruel habit.

8th September 2015

A strange phenomenon occurred this evening while I was giving out healing to a patient. As usual I went into my meditation of passiveness and all seemed tranquil as it usually does. The energies flowing through my arms and fingers seemed to be very strong, a state that is normal to my own sensations.

However, it didn't take long before the energies started to take on a new lease of life, getting stronger and stronger. Frankly, I really enjoyed this feeling, it felt so natural and it was nothing to do with me attempting to increase the energy through the electromagnetic power of stretching out my aura. No, this was something new to me and I had no influence whatsoever.

Suddenly, I became aware of a bright light appearing in the void of tranquillity (noted as the peaceful place where I tend to reside in my meditation) and it felt good. Then a frightful face appeared. I knew this was some sort of malevolency which really should not be there. I ordered this spirit to depart and never to reappear on my patient. I knew that this attachment was the case and it vanished. The feeling that I experienced with my patient was 'as one'. It was like a complete intermingling of the soul, a microcosm of atoms.

Three ancient monks then appeared wearing thick sack-type habits with hoods pulled up over their heads. Their appearance did not alarm me since I knew that I had full control over my meditation. Even so, I still had to convince myself and brought myself back out of this meditation only to find that some of the healers had finished their healing.

I did not allow my patient to know that I had come out of my meditation but felt the need to put a mark on the patient in order to verify that I was in full control of my senses at any given time during the healing session. I continued to give a magnetic healing by enveloping my patient with my own auric energy for just a few seconds.

I quietly brought my patient back to reality; her face was gleaming with happiness. I asked her how she felt. Well, you could have knocked me down with a feather when she replied,

'Oh, Peter, that was wonderful. It seemed as if the both of us just melted into each other's soul. It was extraordinary and yet it felt as if someone was with me. I was told recently that I had an attachment and this person told me that she had got rid of it. I know it has gone now because I feel less anxious, really light, and so refreshed.'

I smiled and said, 'Yes, it was quite an experience, wasn't it? Did you feel a sudden surge of energy at the very end of your healing?'

'Oh yes, it was very strong. It was from the top of my head to the base of my feet,' she replied.

21st September 2015

A great weekend. Saturday's reception party for Steve and Kelly's wedding went off very well. Tina's 60th surprise birthday party was also a great success.

Since my sisters were all at Tina's party I told them that I would look after our mother by taking her to church, which she really loves attending. The medium (Cheryl Y) was from the Black Country. She had a lovely personality that went with her typical accent. Her demonstration was very good as she went around most of the audience with her evidence.

She came around to both my mother and myself bringing in the names of Dad, John, Nan, Ivy, Albert (Mom's dad), Grandma (Mom's mom), Percy, Edith and Stan who was her last partner that used to play the stage with his humour. Cheryl said that there was somebody who enjoyed gardening although it could be any of the above including myself.

Mom had a memory link when her gran used to sit behind her in order to curl her hair with her fingers, then setting the curls with a spray of sugar water. She was also reminded that pipe cleaners were used for the same purpose.

It was unusual to have so many close relatives coming forward, something where time alters life conditions. Usually only one, maybe two relatives will appear, so this makes it very significant. The medium made a good job when she described all of these relatives and I can confirm the facts given are true.

10th October 2015

Yesterday Amanda's open circle turned out to be quite surprising. We were all told to draw a cat and then give it a name. We could also include background objects. I have no idea how my cat looked but I included a tree, the eye of Isis and the sun, even though my own thoughts were quiescent.

We then had to exchange our drawings with the person sat next to us. This exercise was to use psychic powers only, something that concerned me a little since I could not see the drawing in front of me.

However, I just held the paper with my hand over the drawing and started to receive information. Even though I had written down two names, Gemma and Jade, the reading was based on both names in two different ways.

The first was the realisation of the names themselves, which were both taken, and then a spiritualistic and psychological reading which was based within a meaning of precious gems. I gave the example of a pearl because I had written this down as it had come from a living source. Using the word 'gem' I said that jade being a precious stone represents the colour green, the colour given to the heart in the recognition of the chakra system. The heart represents love and it is this love that will see this lady (Stacey) become a spiritual healer. This is all to do with the wantonness of helping others, yet this will occur once her own love has been restored.

The feeling of this lady was a genuine story of how she had survived the tribulations of life which included many aspects of the sorrows and good deeds acquired within that life.

The whole reading ended up in this type of psychic expression but was received with a 'wow effect' from the other students.

Everybody did very well in their psychic readings. Amanda picked out four of the students who had to go onto the stage and give a demonstration of their mediumship. The first three did very well but the fourth gave way because she just wanted the experience of being on stage. While this was acceptable it gave me the opportunity to give my own demonstration to the students, and Amanda agreed that I should go ahead.

I immediately stood up but Amanda said that I should do it from my position as it would take a little time to get me onto the stage.

Because of my blindness it would be impossible to pick out a person to who I should give the message to, so I gave it out to all those listening. The first person within my vision was a naval officer dressed in a white uniform with white cap that had a black shiny peak. He appeared to be about six feet tall, physically fit and good looking. I then noticed a man dressed in green with a white mask hanging from his face, obviously a surgeon who had just come out of the operating theatre. The expression of sorrow on his face suggested that the man he had been operating on had died. An old lady with greying white hair sat in a wheelchair. I fully believed that she accepted her husband would not survive the operation, but nevertheless she gave the surgeon her hand to shake for all of his efforts in trying to save him.

Perhaps quite upsetting, one of the students, who had the same surname as me but was not a relative, said that she could take all of what I had given out. She told everybody that the naval officer was in fact a petty officer, her uncle. The surgeon did indeed attempt to save her grandfather and she also shook his hand and thanked him. The lady in the wheelchair was most definitely her grandmother, her husband having just passed away.

'You are coming on very well, Peter,' Amanda congratulated me, while the person I had just given the message to also thanked me for proving the facts.

The only thing I will criticise is my own deliverance since I rather fumbled through it rather than imagine a public audience in front of me. It looks like I still have a way to go, but there is a lot of improvement to be had.

CHAPTER 8

The Physical Circle

30th January 2016

What a wonderful day I have had today. I attended a private physical circle at our church with a great medium named Janet H. Janet told us that some would experience the production of ectoplasm which a spirit would use to mould wax faces that would appear just in front of our own face. I was one of those who unknowingly could produce ectoplasm as I felt the substance running down from my ears, nose, eyes and mouth. It resembled what I can only describe as sloppy cheese.

The results when each student went into the two cabinets were quite astounding as I listened to the other students talking about what was occurring.

Famous names such as Emily Bronte, Frankie Howard, Tommy Cooper and many more appeared in the masks that were created by the spirit. Sparkling stars jumped around the top of the cabinet, while flashes of coloured light were seen by many of the sitters. It was also noted that some shadows were seen moving about from one cabinet to the other.

Then it was my turn to go into the cabinet. I didn't do anything but meditate, when all of a sudden a warmth around the back of my head signalled the start of something amazing. While the group could clearly see a mask being moulded close to my face in the form of a religious figure, my middle finger on my left hand started to expand and my right hand began to shake in a frenzy. Glowing little stars began to sparkle on top of the cabinet and my throat felt lumpy. I seem to remember saying that my name was Thomas but then my mind became blank.

After my session closed I had to have a little support from one of the students since I could not stand up properly. I guess this was because I must have gone into a slightly deeper trance where my surroundings became closed off to me. Once I had got back safely to my seat I found that a small amount of time had vanished from my memory so I asked one student what I had said.

This is what April, a student medium, relayed to me:

'You started off with an apology for your affliction, then you told us that you were Thomas Becket. You greeted the group and then began to philosophise on not believing all that one reads in books, since truths can and are very often altered by man in his personal opinions. Holy books are one source where man has added his own opinions, so we must be aware of these points.'

Towards the end of the session Janet told us to expect her three spirit children helpers to come out to all of the students in the room but also to expect the rod with plasm ball to be rested in our hands. She also said that relatives of ours will be present and may come to stroke people's faces.

I was already smiling when the plasma ball suddenly appeared in my left hand. It had little weight and made me feel comforted. Then a small hand grasped my hand and started playing with my fingers. It was pure delight as I thanked this small child girl spirit. Finally, both my dad and nan came. Dad spoke of something so I told him he was forgiven now and he should move on in his progression. Nan stroked my face and head very gently which made me tingle with sheer happiness.

This was a wonderful experience to have and it does show that by expanding our knowledge with the ways of the spirits, we have advanced our own progression in this physical life a little more.

The following is the second physical circle that I attended with the same medium as before. While the first circle was mainly a
mixture of both trance talking and face mask construction, this one was how the effects of ectoplasm is used to vary the sequences of face construction.

28th January 2018

I rose early this morning as I had to be in church by 9.30am for the physical circle run by Janet H, a well-known and very good physical and trance medium.

The atmosphere seemed to come alive with energy once the session had begun with eleven of us students plus the medium present. I must admit that a few nerves entered into my physical body through all of the excitement, especially as I would be the first one going into the cabinet. I asked Janet if I could use my digital voice recorder so that I could listen to its contents once back at home. She readily agreed.

All normal light was blotted out with blackout material so that no white light could wreck the proceedings.

A few of the students became a little apprehensive with the darkness that followed after the door was closed and sealed up with tape. However, they soon settled once the dim red light on the small light box was switched on. Darkness does not bother me whatsoever as I am used to living a darkened lifestyle. We were told by the medium that either transfiguration or trance speech is usually decided to be one or the other and, in this case, transfiguration only would be used.

A double cabinet was used so the spirit could walk through one side to the other. Silver stars were placed on both sides so that if the spirit did walk through the dividing section the stars would be blurred out by the spirit's shadow. Other stars were placed on the floor.

As proceedings got underway the physical medium in charge stated that several musical instruments had been placed on the floor. These included a trumpet with reflective yellow strips so that it could be seen more easily in the dark if moved by a spirit. Other instruments included cymbals, a tambourine and rattles. This would enable the sitters to see shadows moving about inside the cabinet.

By the time I entered the cabinet I felt great and all my nerves were gone. Settling in, I soon put myself into a passive state of trance where I felt really comfortable and was able to cut off from the group who were watching with eagerness. A pleasant sense of security crept over me as things began to happen almost immediately, with odd flashes of coloured light and small subtle noises heard.

One seated medium said that she could see a white clothed spirit girl around six years old moving about close to the cabinet. The circle leader agreed that one such girl does come in as she loves to go around and cuddle people in the circle. It was stated that her name was Alice by the group leader Janet.

Strangely, one sitter claimed that her legs had gone quite cold and there was a slight pressure on her shoulders just after her claims of seeing the blonde spirit child. Janet told her that she was being cuddled by Alice. Indeed, shadows and illuminated instruments were noted as being blurred out in places by many sitters.

It must be pointed out at this stage that I was conscious for some of the time although at other times I seemed to drift into a deeper sleep state for short periods. This is one reason that I needed to record this experience so that I could listen to any parts that I may have missed during the transfiguration.

The spirits were already at work because within a very short time transfiguration began on my face with the beginnings of a mask which I did not feel at all. It should be noted that the mask is slightly off the face.

This mask turned into that of a Chinese gentleman with a drooping, thin moustache as one sitter described. I recognised this Chinese spirit gentleman as the spirit surgeon who stood next to me when I was having an operation to remove a blocked artery after having a heart attack in 2011. I'll always remember that experience because the gentleman spirit said, 'No, not that one, man, the other one.'

Energy nodes (equates to a small sack full of energy) appeared on the cheeks, throat and the chest areas. These were the main focal points where the manipulation of ectoplasm of the face and body would be built. Indeed, quite an area on the chest would be enlarged along with the muscles of the arms and neck. This portrays a very muscular person, much like a boxer. An uncle of mine was a boxer named Billy, my father's brother.

It was noted by one sitter that the fingers on my right hand were trembling and jerking uncontrollably which suggested Parkinson's disease. Somebody else was surprised when she saw a male spirit step out of the cabinet as if to check his work. A stroke is suggested as the right arm is seen in shadow which becomes more blurred and the mouth hung down on the right-hand side.

The red light box is suddenly adjusted by the spirit to a much lower setting as it is too bright. This altering of the light tends to be repeated as the situation changes.

On the next occasion the middle finger on the left hand appeared to be growing while the head was seen to be moving as if he wanted to speak. Changes kept on coming as the glistening sparkles on the right side of the earlobe where an earring would have been worn. A pair of spectacles began to form on the mask. However, it was presumed the eyes looked pink which

suggested blood pressure issues according to a few of

the sitters.

These types of conditions and diseases appear to represent particular relatives of my family. Some conditions are unknown by older siblings, but I do recognise certain conditions which are linked with other relatives.

A silver armband was seen on the upper right arm. I presumed that this may have been a size marker for the size of the muscles since it moved a little. I believe this was the height and width to which the moulding of the ectoplasm would take place.

The face then began yet more changes. This time as a female. One of the prominent sitters swore that the face was that of Emma Hardinge Britten, the famous spiritualist medium.

Moving towards the ending of this session, one of the sitting mediums noticed how the right ear seemed to have a cone coming out of it. Suddenly, a voice from the sitting students related to seeing the face of a man on the outside of the cabinet. Light-coloured hair is seen around the face as well as the head.

The medium is now being brought back into reality by the spirit people.

While this account is only brief, it gives the reader some idea of the physical phenomena that takes place. On a scientific basis quite a lot of this account was comparable to my first experience. The flashes of coloured light, movement within the cubicle via the spirit, ectoplasmic mask construction, and relatives coming through all occurred in both events.

Every student had a wonderful time and even the famous singer Amy Winehouse came through one of the other medium students.

Chapter 9

Mediums' Supper

The mediums' supper is one of those events which are held every now and again. There are generally around ten mediums who move around giving readings from a spirit to the six people seated at each table. Afterwards everybody enjoys fish and chips freshly cooked from one of the local fish and chip shops.

I don't usually make recordings of these events, but if proof is to be verified that life continues after our mortal death, then this is proof positive that our mediums are the communicational voice for spirits in the spirit dimension.

My mother, sister Tina and partner Ruth all joined me at the meeting. I don't know who the other two ladies were but they also got their own readings which I did not record.

This is the actual transcript that I wrote down. There are two separate mediums who came to our table, yet I found them both displaying their own style of humour and emotions.

Medium - 'I feel your husband was quite a loving man. It's as if I want to touch you and put my arms around you. Do you understand? Not very passionate, but if he walked around you he would touch your arms. It would have been enough. Okay?'
Mom - 'Yes.'
Medium - 'Robert, you know this name?'
Mom - 'No.'
Pete - 'I can take that name.'
Medium - 'And you can take Pete as well?'
Pete - 'That's my name.'
Mom - 'I've got so many!'

Medium - 'And Stuart, I have to say the name Stuart.'
Pete - 'Yes, I can take that.'
Medium - 'And Michael please.'
Pete - 'Yes.'
Mom - 'I can't really take any of those.'
Medium - 'I feel as if I'm talking to all three of you (Mom, Tina, Peter). Is that alright?'
Mom - 'Yes, that's alright.'
Medium - 'Pete, you'll understand somebody having tattoos?'
Pete - 'Yes.'
Medium - 'Thank you. It's a man having a bird tattoo, a swallow.'
Pete - 'Yes.'
Medium - 'Thank you. You can take Margaret as well?'
Pete - 'Yes.'
Medium - 'Thank you, and I've got to give you horses, but I've got to give you beautiful visions of horses. Do you understand?'
Pete - 'Yes.'
Medium - 'Thank you, and it's as if it's in your mind's eye you see lovely white stallions. Do you understand me?'
Pete - 'Yes, thank you.'
Medium - Like galloping across and I want to put wings on them, and I've just got to give you or let you know that the spirit world understands your visions. Do you paint?'
Pete - 'Thank you and yes, I used to before I went blind. But I was always artistic.'
Medium - 'Oh, artistic yes, but your visions, your colours that you see are absolutely wonderful, that's what I've got to give you here.'
Pete - 'Thank you.'
Medium - 'Have you got a stick?'
Pete - 'Yes.'
Medium - 'Do you tap your stick sometimes?'
Pete - 'Well, yes, I suppose I do sometimes.'

Ruth - 'Yes he does.'
Medium - 'Does he tap his stick at you? I've got bang, bang, bang, as if he's tapping his stick at you.'
Ruth- 'Yes, he says where are you? Ha ha.' (Everybody laughs.)
Medium - 'I don't feel as if this is the first dog you've had.'
Pete - 'No.'
Medium - 'Thank you. I feel as if there's been another dog.'
Pete - 'Yes.'
Medium - 'Okay, is this dog black?'
Pete - 'Yes.'
Medium - 'And was the other dog you had brown?'
Pete - 'Well, the other dogs were gold and yellow.'
Medium - 'I should be telling you because you can't see (laughter). Did this dog have some length to its fur?'
Pete - 'I did have one pet dog which had length to its coat.'
Medium - 'Thank you, a beautiful shape to the lovely tail. Stood like a show dog. Do you understand me?'
Pete - 'Yes he was.'
Medium - 'And another golden Labrador with very short hair, pink nose.'
Pete - 'Yes.'
Medium - 'And a pink tongue always hanging out, but one of them was one who kept pinching food.'
Pete - 'Yes.'
Medium - 'Yes, and apparently they're trained not to pinch food but the temptation was too much for him. If there was a biscuit on the coffee table he would have, it wouldn't he? Oh yes, he would have it, but it's as if there wasn't anybody watching him and he didn't care. All his training went out of the window when it came to food, didn't it?'
Pete - 'Sounds about right.'
Medium - 'Very obedient dog except for the biscuits,

especially the pink wafer biscuits, and also I've got to give you Jammie Dodgers, yes?'
Pete - 'Oh yes, I still love both of these.'
Medium - 'Yes, and Bourbon biscuits. These dogs are coming through with lots of love, in fact I can see two dogs around you but I'm also sensing the other dog. It's sitting up, but I can see the dogs around, yes?'
Pete - 'Thank you.'
Medium - 'Thank you, and can I say God bless you. I'll come to you now, Tina. I've got Nan in the spirit world.'
Tina - 'Yes.'
Medium - 'Well it's not Mom is it? (Laughter.) Sorry. I think you were quite young when Nan passed over, but you've got memories, yes?'
Tina - 'Yes.'
Medium - 'I want to talk about her skin. I feel as if it's quite dehydrated, quite dry when she passed over.'
Tina - 'Yes.'
Medium - 'Thank you, and I've got quite a few age spots on her hands. Brown marks are what she is showing me.'
Tina - 'Yes.'
Medium - 'And she lived in a terraced house?'
Tina - 'Was it terraced (asking me)?'
Medium - 'Thank you, and I've got a table by the back window.'
Tina - 'Yes.'
Medium - 'And it would have been a kitchen table and she sits down and looks down the back garden? It's a big old sash window that looks out, yes?'
Tina - 'Yes.'
Medium - 'I've got a big staircase. Do you understand?'
Tina - 'Yes.'
Medium - 'And while there was quite a lot of light upstairs it would be quite cold. She's showing me the old warming pans for the beds and she's talking about warming up a brick.

Wrapping up a brick and putting it at the end of the bed.'
Tina - 'Yes.'
Medium - 'This lady lived in Birmingham because she's talking about the bombing there. Yes, and I've also got to give you Flood Street (everybody talks) and Spark Hill.'
Mom - 'Yes.'
Medium - 'You can take Bill please and Owen? I'm not sure whether this is a first name or last name, and I've got to give you Bristol Street Motors in Birmingham.'
Mom - 'Oh yes.'
Medium - 'Because somebody would have worked there or bought a motor from there.'
Mom - 'Yes.'
Medium - 'And he's talking about the eleven hundred here as well. Somebody had an eleven hundred.'
Mom - Yes, he did. (Peter had one but Mom believes it was Stan's.)
Medium - 'Thank you. And I've got one that's a plum colour and one that was a brown colour.'
Mom - 'Yes.'
Medium - 'That's what he's showing me here, and he's also showing me an Avenger and I've pulled the number plate down on one car. I think it's a Zephyr I'm looking at here and the petrol cap was behind the number plate. Do you understand me?'
Mom - 'Yes I do.'
Medium - 'I've got to give you the memory of that and also going out on holiday as a day trip?'
Mom - 'Yes.'
Medium - 'Get into the car, car full six o'clock in the morning, five thirty in the morning, taking off, and I'm not sure whether this is. Is it Wales I'm going?'
Mom - 'Yes.'
Medium - 'I'm also going down to Weston and Burnham on Sea.'
Mom - 'Yes, we almost lived there.'

Medium - 'Burnham on Sea I've got everything in there, one of those inflatable beach balls. It was that windy whenever we go and whoosh, the ball's gone again. I've just got to bring you the memory of those days and you're such a busy thing on these days out. You've got bread and butter and some rolls there. You're sitting against a wall making sandwiches here. Do you understand me?'
Mom - 'Yes.'
Medium - 'They look like ham and tomato. They're white rolls but they are so nice. You're spreading the butter here, ooh, don't drop them, don't get them near the sand, and I've got little kids here eating them. Do you understand please?'
Mom - 'Oh yes.' (Laughter.)
Medium - 'I've also got the flask of tea for the adults, yes? Dad's got the deck chair because he's done the driving and he's sat there with a tweed jacket on. It's not beach stuff, eh? I know that he would have liked the Morris at some time because he's talking about the Morris.'
Mom - 'Yes.'
Medium - 'Thank you, so I don't know how everything got in the boot of that car because you've got everything in it, the picnic, the lot, and just happy, happy holidays. Just memories of those. I've got to give you liquorice?'
Mom - 'Yes, that's me.'
Medium - 'Thanks, and Liquorice allsorts and Bertie Basset's and somebody loves Thornton's toffee as well, somebody loving toffee. I'm going to the market here to buy toffee and I see a hammer breaking it up from a tray.'
Mom - 'Oh yes, we used to do that.'
Medium - 'I've got to give you banana toffee as well, Ernie, you can take Ernie.'
Mom - 'I've never heard of Ernie.'
Medium - 'And I've got to say before I go that our day trip was
never finished unless we stopped for fish and chips before

you set off back, yes?'
Mom - 'Yes.'
Medium - 'You're going somewhere, always having loads of salt and vinegar, sitting there and the kids are falling asleep. Do you understand me?'
Mom - 'Oh yes, lovely.'
Medium - 'He just wanted them to make you happy and the smile on your face tells me that you are happy. God bless and thank you.'

Next Medium

Medium - 'I've got your mother here and she's placed a rhubarb pie in front of you. She says that you were a greedy little bugger.'
Mom - 'Oh yes, I don't know about that.' (Laughter.)
Medium - 'She said that you loved your puddings and things like that. Nice woman your mom, very good. She's got a good heart and she'll give anything to anybody. Are you related to him over there (meaning me - Pete)?'
Mom - 'He's my son.'
Medium - 'Never, you don't look old enough to have that lot.'
Mom - 'I've got twelve.'
Medium - 'You look younger than him!' (Laughter.)
Mom - 'Oh, don't tell him that.'
Pete - 'I love you too, Pauline, and I thought you were my friend.'
Medium - 'I won't. Friends, we're the only ones that you've got! As I said, she was a good-natured woman. So, you can all listen to this because I'll come to all of you, you know, kill all of you with one stone. Know what I mean? So, she goes around all of you. Would you have known where there are a bunch of love letters that are kept in a box?'
Mom - 'No, I haven't got any letters.'

Medium - 'Did you ever have any love letters?'
Mom - 'Myself, yes.'
Medium - 'Did you keep them in a box?'
Mom - 'Yes.'
Medium - 'Well, I've just said...' (Much laughter.)
Medium - 'Oh roll on me fish.' (Medium is frustrated but joking.) 'Have you still got em?'
Mom - 'Err... no, yes, no.'
Medium - 'Why not?'
Mom - 'It's was a long time ago.'
Medium - 'Can you remember what he said? Was it all about sex?'
Mom - 'Err... No, (laughing) you didn't talk about that.'
Medium - 'Well they didn't do it in them days.'
We all said - 'She's got twelve kids!' (All erupt with laughter.)
Medium - 'Listen, did you know the name Phyllis?'
Mom - 'Err... no.'
Medium - 'Yes you did. When you were young did you work?'
Mom - 'Yes.'
Medium - 'With this Phyllis did you ever go cleaning?'
Mom - 'No.'
Medium - 'Who used to go cleaning?'
Mom - 'My auntie perhaps?'
Medium - 'Well somebody who used to go cleaning is here, and it might be her but she's saying you both knew a Phyllis. When you have a cup of tea you might remember her. And who's Michael?'
Pete - 'My son is named Michael.'
Medium - 'Has Michael needed some help in some way?'
Pete - 'Not to my knowledge.'
Medium - 'Well, he's going to come to you, Mother (looking at Ruth).'
Ruth - 'I'm not his mom.'
Medium - 'You're his stepmother, aren't you?'

Ruth - 'Well, I suppose so.'
Medium - 'Well you watch him come for something.'
Ruth - 'Right, okay, yes.'
Medium - 'Billy, who's Billy?'
Everyone discusses this and can all link with a Billy who is probably Tracie's partner.
Medium - 'Did you ever know anybody working on the markets?'
Everyone seems to agree - Stan most likely.
Medium - 'I've got someone here selling goods off a market stall.'
I remind Mom that Stan did this. Mom agrees.
Medium - 'I think they are all dead here… He's the only one with a memory.' (Mom's laughing and Pauline's pulling funny faces and cackling.) 'Now, one of you lot… your husband's here, he wants to say hello to you and say he loves you very much. Thank you for what you did for him, he said. Aww, so you must have looked after him, helped him, did you?'
Mom - 'Yes.'
Medium - 'Cos he said he's waiting for you over there. He's doing this (Pauline's doing a funny clip, clopping sound) so you can get away from this lot.'
(Mom is laughing madly saying, 'He's not, is he?')

The tape runs out at this point but Pauline eventually says 'God bless' after much laughing.

Next Medium

Medium - 'I want to go for a drink okay. Come on, I'm going to take you out.'
Mom - 'Yes, okay.'
Medium - 'Now there's no issue with this lad, he won't go down that line at all, alright?'
Mom - 'Yes.'

Medium - 'He wants everything upfront, okay? He's just come to you and said, "We're not having anything like that so stop those tears," and I just feel that he wants to uplift you and brighten up your life, okay? He's laughing here and I think he's trying to pull my leg.'
Mom - 'That's about right, he was always doing that.'
Medium - 'He's talking about a photograph of himself in shorts as a boy, and he's saying, "*Look at me, look at me, look what I'm wearing*," okay?'
Mom - 'Yes.'
Medium - 'He's drawing me the letter D. Would you understand this?'
Mom - 'No.' (We point out that it could be Diana his daughter.)
Medium - 'He's also talking about Joe - Joseph.'
Mom - 'No.'
Medium - 'He's talking about someone in the spirit world saying that he's met up with someone of that name, okay?' Ruth enquires if it could be John.
Medium - 'I'll see if I can get something to back it up, okay?' (The medium starts laughing.) 'Tell her that I'll take her to the pub, that's what he's saying. It's as if he wants to put all the attention on you at the moment because he's saying that you feel all alone and that he's very much around you at home. He keeps giving me white feathers as well, and I don't know if you know that it's one of my beliefs when I am talking to the spirit world that I tend to feel a lot of feathers, what my father calls "pigeon feathers". They just seem to be around all he time.'
Tina - 'I found a feather and this was a small white one.'
Medium - 'They're like the little white ones, they're appearing on your feet. Err… the way you're walking, and it's as if they're appearing on your feet, on your pathway. And appearing
in your home. Just watch out for it because it's a beautiful thing.'

Mom - 'Okay.'
Medium - 'I'm just coming to you, sir. Do you know what it's like walking into cobwebs?'
Pete - 'Oh yes, I do.'
Medium - 'You can feel them on your face, this is what he's trying to create around you alright, so if you have experienced that watch out for it because he's trying to create this for you.'
Pete - 'Thank you.'
Medium starts singing and laughs.
Medium - 'This man is singing. It's just to let you know that he's still around.'
Mom - 'Thank you.'

In tribute to our beloved mother born 17th February 1927 and passed 28th December 2019.

Printed in Great Britain
by Amazon